LIVING FEARLESS

GUIDED JOURNAL

EXCHANGING THE LIES OF THE WORLD
FOR THE LIBERATING TRUTH OF GOD

JAMIE WINSHIP

a division of Baker Publishing Group
Grand Rapids, Michigan

© 2025 by Jamie Winship

Published by Revell
a division of Baker Publishing Group
Grand Rapids, Michigan
RevellBooks.com

Printed in the United States of America

All rights reserved. No part of this publication may be reproduced, stored in a retrieval system, or transmitted in any form or by any means—for example, electronic, photocopy, recording—without the prior written permission of the publisher. The only exception is brief quotations in printed reviews.

Library of Congress Cataloging-in-Publication Data
Names: Winship, Jamie, 1959– author.
Title: Living fearless guided journal : exchanging the lies of the world for the liberating truth of God / Jamie Winship.
Description: Grand Rapids, Michigan : Revell, a division of Baker Publishing Group, [2025] | Includes bibliographical references.
Identifiers: LCCN 2024028079 | ISBN 9780800746896 (paper) | ISBN 9781493449712 (ebook)
Subjects: LCSH: Truth—Religious aspects—Christianity. | Truthfulness and falsehood—Religious aspects—Christianity.
Classification: LCC BT50 .W478 2025 | DDC 231/.042—dc23/eng/20240716
LC record available at https://lccn.loc.gov/2024028079

Unless otherwise indicated, Scripture quotations are from the Holy Bible, New International Version®, NIV®. Copyright © 1973, 1978, 1984, 2011 by Biblica, Inc.® Used by permission of Zondervan. All rights reserved worldwide. www.zondervan.com. The "NIV" and "New International Version" are trademarks registered in the United States Patent and Trademark Office by Biblica, Inc.®

Scripture quotations labeled AMP are from the Amplified Bible. Copyright © 2015 by The Lockman Foundation. Used by permission. www.lockman.org

Scripture quotations labeled AMPC are from the Amplified Bible. Copyright © 1954, 1958, 1962, 1964, 1965, 1987 by The Lockman Foundation. Used by permission. www.lockman.org

Scripture quotations labeled ESV are from The Holy Bible, English Standard Version® (ESV®). Copyright © 2001 by Crossway, a publishing ministry of Good News Publishers. Used by permission. All rights reserved. ESV Text Edition: 2016

Scripture quotations labeled KJV are from the King James Version of the Bible.

Scripture quotations labeled MSG are from *The Message*. Copyright © 1993, 2002, 2018 by Eugene H. Peterson. Used by permission of NavPress. All rights reserved. Represented by Tyndale House Publishers.

Scripture quotations labeled NASB are from the (NASB®) New American Standard Bible®. Copyright © 1960, 1971, 1977, 1995, 2020 by The Lockman Foundation. Used by permission. All rights reserved. www.lockman.org

Scripture quotations labeled NKJV are from the New King James Version®. Copyright © 1982 by Thomas Nelson. Used by permission. All rights reserved.

Scripture quotations labeled NLT are from the *Holy Bible*, New Living Translation. Copyright © 1996, 2004, 2015 by Tyndale House Foundation. Used by permission of Tyndale House Publishers, Carol Stream, Illinois 60188. All rights reserved.

Scripture quotations labeled TPT are from The Passion Translation®. Copyright © 2017, 2018, 2020 by Passion & Fire Ministries, Inc. Used by permission. All rights reserved. ThePassionTranslation.com.

Portions of this text are from *Living Fearless: Exchanging the Lies of the World for the Liberating Truth of God* (Grand Rapids: Revell, 2022).

The names and details of the people and situations described in this book have been changed or presented in composite form in order to ensure the privacy of those with whom the author has worked.

Cover design by Marc Whitaker, MTWdesign

Baker Publishing Group publications use paper produced from sustainable forestry practices and post-consumer waste whenever possible.

25 26 27 28 29 30 31   7 6 5 4 3 2

Contents

What This Journal Is About   5
How This Journal Works   9

Session 1   Abide to Thrive   15
Session 2   Conversations with Jesus   27
Session 3   Vocation Flows from Identity   41
Session 4   Unified and Unique   55
Session 5   Thriving in the Now   67
Session 6   What's in a Name?   79
Session 7   The False Self   91
Session 8   Confession: The Start of Transformation   105
Session 9   Learning to *Hear*   121
Session 10   Stepping Out in Faith   135
Session 11   When We Need Wisdom   149
Session 12   Discovering Your Mission   163

Final Note   177
Confession Pages   179
Hear and Put into Practice   187

What This Journal Is About

Recently, while I was meeting with a group of upper-level leaders of a large organization, I shared with the women and men about how from a person's truest identity flows something known as a vocation. Since this was a secular organization, I stopped short of using words and phrases like *the abundant life*, *calling*, *abiding*, and *in Christ*, but those were certainly what I was getting at.

I explained that a person's vocation, though certainly encompassing what they do for money, is far more than what we understand as "a job." It is what they were made for, the way they were wired to show up in any given situation—their purpose in life but also their way of living most free in any given moment.

I expressed to them that living in your vocation—one that flows from your truest self—is the only real way to thrive in this life.

After my presentation, one of the men in the group came up to me and explained that his role with this organization pushed him to live outside of what he felt to be his identity. He was constantly trying to mold himself into someone who could thrive where he was, trying to build his vocation around what he was doing rather than who he actually was.

"I wonder if you'd be happier doing something else," I said as gently as I could.

He nodded as the weight of these words sunk in—his whole life would have to change—but he also seemed to sense the truth in them.

As the man walked away, another member of the leadership team approached, having overheard our conversation. "Thank you for saying that," he said sincerely. "He has seemed out of place with us for a long time, and we didn't know how to handle the situation."

It wasn't that the man was disliked or didn't do a good job at his work. On the contrary, he seemed to be a valuable member of the team, someone his colleagues cared about deeply. But everyone could sense that he was out of place, not living as one whose vocation (what he was here to do) flowed from his identity (who he was meant to be).

I felt compassion rising up within me. How many of us feel this way in our lives? How many of God's children feel like they have to be someone else just to fit in where they happen to be? Is that really the abundant life Jesus has planned for us? Is that really thriving?

Over the years, as I have presented this material to CEOs, politicians, religious leaders (of various faiths), and my Christian sisters and brothers, I have found that most of us not only misunderstand who we are but, because of that, also severely misinterpret what we have been put on this earth to do.

We follow all sorts of idols—money, sex, glory, success, worldly significance, control, power, people-pleasing, and more—believing them to give us the keys to experiencing fulfillment and purpose in life. But like drinking salt water, these only leave us more dried out than before.

But what if we started to take seriously Jesus's promise to give us *life to the full* (see John 10:10)? What if we actually believed that we could have access (at least in part) to that life in the now? How might that change how we approach our days here on this earth?

When I finished my book *Living Fearless*, I knew from the response that there were so many people out there thirsting to understand and embrace their true God-given identity. But the natural question always came: "Well, what do I do now that I am embracing more fully who I really am?" I certainly touched on this topic in my book, but I found that I wasn't able to answer this question as adequately as I would have liked.

From that need, this journal began to take shape. I wanted to offer much of the identity work that I explain in *Living Fearless* but in a way that is more interactive so that whether you have read the book or not, you can come to this journal where you are and find more of who God created you to be.

I also wanted to spend a greater amount of time on the implications of this true identity, what it means when put into action. In response to that, this journal also spends a great deal of time helping those who engage with it to better understand the vocation(s) that will naturally flow from who they were created to be.

Just imagine for a minute what that might be like, to understand to a greater and greater degree who you are and what you are here to do as you engage more and more with your Creator and Redeemer. How might that change your life?

Over and over again, I have seen how embracing these—your true identity and vocation in Christ—allows followers of Jesus to take seriously the abundant life in the here and now. I have seen and experienced firsthand how this leads those courageous enough to step out in faith—by the power and grace of Jesus—to a life of wonderful and incredible thriving.

That is what the *Living Fearless Guided Journal* is all about.

How This Journal Works

In this interactive journal, I will walk you through concepts that are vital for you to experience the thriving life Jesus intends for you. This material is intentionally set up as a guided experience, an opportunity for you to connect with Jesus around the areas of your identity and vocation in Christ. To that end, the impact of what Jesus will do is intended to bleed far beyond the edge of the page and into your mind, heart, life, and relationships.

Thought-provoking questions, along with spaces for writing, are consistently provided to encourage prayer and reflection throughout. Feel free to utilize these invitations in ways that work best for you, but I encourage you to make the most of these spaces as you engage with God and lean into the interactive nature of this journal. When we are open to Jesus in these areas, he will transform our understanding of who we are (our identity) and what we are here to do (our vocation).

Your time in this journal will be divided into a series of sessions, with each session designed to unpack a key concept and help you engage with Jesus in light of the material. Sessions will begin with a short introduction made up of content curated and adapted from my book *Living Fearless*. (Again, you don't have to have read the book, and if you have, I trust you will find this journal supplemental rather than redundant.)

Then I will lead you through four sections, as defined in my book, that reflect the key aspects of abiding in Jesus: Attention, Awareness, Annunciation, and Action. I recommend completing an entire session in one sitting.

Here is what you can expect from the four sections of each session:

Attention

One of the most important parts of abiding in Jesus is intentionally giving our attention over to him regularly. Paying attention to Jesus—the things he is saying to us—is how a life of thriving begins to be unlocked within us and in our spirit. Because of this, we will pause in each session to recalibrate our attention to God and attune to the things he desires us to see, hear, and notice.

In the "Attention" section of each session, you will engage with a passage of Scripture and some information around that passage to help attune you to God and his truth. These passages have writing space after them, offering you ample room to engage with the Scripture. You will slowly read through each passage three times, considering what words, phrases, or ideas God might be highlighting for you.

After the passage and related reading, you will ask Jesus some questions and then write down the first thing that comes to mind. This is about building confidence in recognizing Jesus's voice when he talks to you. Don't be afraid to make a mistake. Just remember that God's voice, as revealed through Scripture, is always rooted in love for you and love for others.

So, in these spaces, just practice by writing down the first thing you sense. Write it down right away. Don't wait. Don't analyze it, and don't question it or try to figure out whether it's coming from you or God. Just write down what is on your mind or in your heart.

At first, you may not understand what you've written, and that's okay. Many times when Jesus spoke, people didn't know what he meant. For now, practice saying out loud what you hear or see in your mind or sense in your heart. The more you practice this—while also spending time in Scripture and Christ-centered community—the more you will be able to recognize God's voice when you hear it.

Awareness

The next step is to foster a continual posture of attention throughout our lives, which for our purposes we will call awareness. In the "Awareness" sections, our goal will be to become more and more open to the movement of Jesus's Spirit in and around us as we move through our day-to-day interactions and experiences.

In each session, I will guide you through a reflective exercise in which you prayerfully consider the last twenty-four hours, allowing Jesus to speak to you about your day and highlight where and how he was present with you. To do this, you will consider the three parts of the last twenty-four hours (morning, afternoon, and evening) and prayerfully answer two questions for each part of your day:

- What situations, events, experiences, thoughts, and feelings is Jesus highlighting for me?
- What does Jesus want to say to me about what he has highlighted?

Then you will conclude the "Awareness" section by considering all that Jesus highlighted and asking him how he was present with you and how he wants you to notice him in similar situations in the future.

Annunciation

As we build a consistent rhythm of abiding in Christ—paying attention to and becoming aware of the movements of Jesus—it is important that we regularly allow Jesus to speak to us about our identity. There are parts of our internal self that grow from a place of brokenness and insecurity. This false identity leads us to live from a place of fear in our lives and causes us to compete, compare, self-protect, and self-promote in our interactions with God and others. Jesus wants to highlight these areas of the false self for us and exchange them for the true self that he created and redeemed us to be.

In the "Annunciation" section of each session, I will walk you through this process as you prayerfully ask Jesus to help you put down aspects of your false identity and pick up more and more of your true self in Christ. We will do this by going through a series of questions and prayers with Jesus, again writing out the first thing he brings to your heart or mind.

Afterward, you will ask Jesus for a word or phrase that he wants to leave you with for that day about your true identity. This is something you can hold on to that will ground you and bring you back to the aspect of your true self that Jesus is awakening within you.

Action

At the end of each session, you will be left with a unique exercise or activity that is intended to encourage action that flows from the true self Jesus is awakening within you. As this journal progresses, I pray you will discover more of who you are (your identity) and, in turn, more of what you are here to do (your vocation). This "Action" section will vary from session to session, but the aim will be the same: to help you to create space in your life for the outflowing of your identity through your actions and vocation.

Finally, every session will end with a few questions for further reflection or discussion. You can engage with these questions on your own or with another person or group of people who are also going through this journal.

As we move forward together, I encourage you more than anything to lean into the Lord Jesus—to trust that he will enliven my words with power. Like a length of wire waiting to be electrified, my words will do very little for you apart from the Spirit of Jesus. Every word, thought, activity, and prayer is intended to point to him, the only one through whom your identity and vocation can come to life within you. I pray that you will allow this journal to be an invitation into what only he can do, an invitation to abide in the only true source of a life abundant.

It is only then that we will thrive.

SESSION 1
ABIDE TO THRIVE

As a young police officer in the mid-1980s, I started to get a taste for what it meant to really thrive in that aspect of my life. In 1985, I was even named Police Officer of the Year. It was safe to say I was thriving in my role. I owed my success as a police officer to four persons: the Father, Son, and Holy Spirit . . . and the Master Police Officer known as the Troll.

The Troll was one of the most feared training officers in the police department. As a rookie, I had heard that what the Troll lacked in interpersonal skills and human kindness he made up for in making the life of a new recruit a nightmare. Rumor had it, he would proudly smirk as the beleaguered rookies he was assigned to train decided to forgo completing their training, instead turning in their gun and badge to seek employment somewhere else—anywhere else.

For my first year as a police officer, I was assigned to train with the Troll, to spend hours upon hours with this notoriously tough man. He would own my life for the next twelve months and would determine my vocational future.

On our first shift together, he said to me, "I've got one simple rule for you, Rookie. For the time you and I will be abiding together, you are not allowed to talk at all unless I give you permission, and that will be seldom. Do you understand that?"

I nodded my head, but I was thinking, *Did the Troll just use the word* abiding? *Did this great nemesis of the neophyte cop employ the word* abiding *because he is a fan of the Bible or* The Big Lebowski?

"The reason you will not be talking," the Troll continued, "is because when you are talking, I am not talking. And when I am not talking, you are not listening. And if you are not listening, then you are not learning. So your goal for the next year, if you remain with me that long, is to keep your mouth shut, listen, and learn. If you can do that, you might live through this. Got it?"

I nodded my head again, but I was thinking, *Did I just hear a really good sermon on prayer?*

In the year that followed, I spent fifty weeks of four-day, ten-hour shifts with the first real discipler of my life. Although the Troll was not a Christ follower, he understood the art of discipleship better than anyone I had met previously.

As I abided—stayed, remained, persisted—with the Troll, I learned what it meant to thrive in my role as a police officer. By sharing in his life as a police officer—being in his presence; watching him; learning his pace, manner, and the subtle intricacies of being one who served and protected the public; listening to him; being open to his instruction (and perhaps more importantly, his questions)—I learned more than I ever could have through a training course.

It was life-on-life growth, and it provided me with the best example of discipleship that I have ever seen. A relationship of abiding is the means by which Jesus leads his disciples (you and me) into the life of fullness and thriving that he has always planned for us. If we are going to thrive in this life, it is essential that we start to understand and unpack what it really means to abide in Jesus.

> When you think of the word *abide*, what comes to mind? If you had to, how would you define the word?

Attention

Slowly and intentionally read through the following passage three times. As you do, consider what words, phrases, or ideas God might be highlighting for you. Circle or underline what stands out to you, then answer the questions after the passage.

> I am the true vine, and My Father is the vinedresser. Every branch in Me that does not bear fruit He takes away; and every branch that bears fruit He prunes, that it may bear more fruit. You are already clean because of the word which I have spoken to you. Abide in Me, and I in you. As the branch cannot bear fruit of itself, unless it abides in the vine, neither can you, unless you abide in Me.
>
> I am the vine, you are the branches. He who abides in Me, and I in him, bears much fruit; for without Me you can do nothing. (John 15:1–5 NKJV)

After reading the passage above, what most stands out to you? What parts are confusing to you? What questions do you have?

In the passage, Jesus tells us simply, "Abide in Me, and I in you." The word translated *abide* in this passage is the Greek word *menō*. This verb was regularly used in reference to place, meaning to stay or to remain somewhere, often longer than was originally planned. The word could also denote a level of presence of a person or situation, or it could mean to continue, persist, live on, endure, or be held.

In The Passion Translation, verse 4 says, "So you must remain in life-union with me, for I remain in life-union with you." This abiding life-union with Jesus is available to us today and includes all the fullness of the Godhead; spiritual fruitfulness; the fullness of the words, love, and joy of the Father; answered prayer; and the glory and honor of God.[1]

According to Dr. John Piper, abiding, in this context, is the act of receiving and trusting all that God has and is for us in Christ.[2] Abiding is not something that we can do simply by worshiping on a Sunday morning or learning in a Bible study. This is a life-on-life connection with Jesus, a relationship lived and experienced in real time.

Eugene Peterson paraphrases verse 4 this way: "Live in me. Make your home in me just as I do in you" (MSG). Just imagine yourself for a moment making your home in Jesus, in his presence, in his love, in his

---

1. John 15:1, 5, 7, 8, 9, 11, 26.
2. John Piper, "What Does It Mean to 'Abide in Christ'?," September 22, 2017, in *Ask Pastor John*, podcast, MP3 audio, 12:16, https://www.desiringgod.org/interviews/what-does-it-mean-to-abide-in-christ.

will. Now imagine him doing the same—making his home, his dwelling place, the place where he would choose to be more than anywhere else—in you.

This is what I mean by a life-on-life connection with Jesus and what is meant by abiding. It is only in this context that we can truly start to understand who we are and what we are here to do. It is only when we abide that we can actually start to thrive in the life we have been given.

> Jesus, in light of or beyond the passage above, what is the most important thing you want to say to me right now?

> Jesus, why are you saying this to me? What do you want me to understand or see differently about myself, you, or the world?

Awareness

Prayerfully consider the last twenty-four hours—morning, afternoon, and evening—allowing yourself to become aware of Jesus's presence with you throughout the day. Chart out your day below.

	What situations, events, experiences, thoughts, and feelings is Jesus highlighting for me?	What does Jesus want to say to me about what he has highlighted?
MORNING		
AFTERNOON		
EVENING		

> Considering what Jesus highlighted for you above, ask him how he was present with you throughout your day. How might he want you to notice him in similar situations in the future?

Annunciation

Ask Jesus the following questions, and write out the first thing he brings to your heart or mind.

> Jesus, what aspect of my false identity am I holding on to that you want to highlight for me today?

> Jesus, how does that aspect of my false identity lead me to live from a place of fear? How does it awaken in me the desire to compete, compare, self-protect, and/or self-promote?

Pray the following prayer over yourself, lifting up and releasing to Jesus the aspect of your false self he has revealed to you.

Lord Jesus, as I give this aspect of my false identity to you, cleanse me of that lie and the fear it produces. I give it to you now, Christ Jesus. By the power of your life, death, and resurrection, I leave my burdens at the cross and take up your protection from and silencing of the enemy and all the false things in my life. As you bear this false identity in your own flesh, please exchange it within me for my true identity in you.

Next, ask Jesus the following questions about your true identity, again writing out the first thing he brings to your heart or mind.

> Jesus, in light of that false identity, would you speak back to me the name, or identity, that you call me? What do you want to reveal to me about my true identity today? What do you want to announce over me?

Jesus, how would understanding this aspect of my true identity produce in me courage rather than fear? How would embracing this truth about who I am allow me to thrive in my life?

Pray the following prayer over yourself, holding in your heart and mind the aspect of your true self that Jesus has revealed to you.

Lord Jesus, when I give you my shame, you give me back honor. When I give you my guilt, you give me back innocence. When I give you my fear, you give me back power and authority. By the power of the cross, I claim the beautiful exchange of identity that you make possible for me. In your beautiful voice, Lord, I embrace the aspect of my true identity that you have made known to me today. Thank you for what you call me.

Jesus, what one word or phrase do you want to leave me with today about my true identity?

Action

First, take the word or phrase about your true self that Jesus left you with for today (taken from the previous "Annunciation" section) and write it in the space provided below.

Next, prayerfully consider what sort of fruit (the external outflow of this internal identity shift) might naturally flow from abiding in Jesus and embracing the aspect of your true identity that you have received from him today. How might Jesus use this new identity to impact your life (thoughts, feelings, actions, interactions, relationships, etc.), helping you to better thrive?

Write some words or phrases in the grapes below.

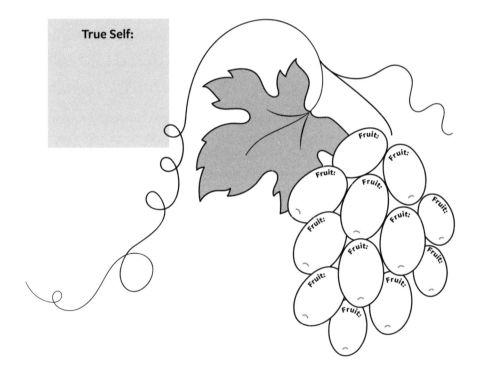

For Discussion or Further Reflection

Describe a time when you felt at home in Jesus's presence. What did you notice about how you were opening up to Jesus at that time?

When reading John 15:1–5, what do you notice about abiding in Christ? What does Jesus reveal to you about what it means to abide?

Where in your life have you succeeded in abiding in Christ? Where do you most struggle?

What is one practical way you can practice abiding in Jesus this week?

SESSION 2

CONVERSATIONS WITH JESUS

One morning I called a ride share company to go to the airport. I wanted to have a conversation with the driver, so I got in the front seat when the car arrived. The driver seemed surprised, as if that wasn't the right *formula* for riding in a hired vehicle when you're alone.

There is a theory in the study of language formation called formulaic language formation. Essentially, to save time and energy, societies develop predictable patterns of communication and interaction for the situations that they encounter on a day-to-day basis. One party will start by engaging the other in an appropriate, predictable manner, and in turn the other party responds in the appropriate, predictable manner. Without even noticing, we use language formulas all the time, though most of these formulas vary from culture to culture.

Having lived in the Arab world for years and years, I learned to always ride in the front seat with a taxi driver. If you get behind the driver, it means you don't like him, so you always get in the front seat. And if you want him to know that you really want to talk to him, you grab his leg. But not with your left hand, because that's unclean, so you have to reach across and grab his leg with your right hand.

Being well steeped in this cultural formula, after I jumped in the front seat of the ride share, I said hello and reached over to grab the guy's leg. Startled, he jumped back against his door and said, "What are you doing?" Clearly I was using the wrong formula of communication for my Americanized driver.

"How are you doing?" I asked, attempting to recover from my mistake.

"You're going to the airport?" he replied.

"Yeah."

"Where are you going?" he asked.

"Salt Lake City."

"Do they have good restaurants there?"

"I don't know. Maybe. I don't know if people fly to Salt Lake City to eat. It's known for other stuff, not necessarily restaurants."

We had gotten back on track, engaging in a formulaic conversation that my driver seemed comfortable with—predictable questions and responses—but it really didn't matter what either of us was saying. Neither of us actually cared. The goal was to get through the interaction with as little thought or connection as possible.

And therein lies the problem when we use formulaic communication in real relationships. It does not lead to authentic or dynamic connections with others. Formulaic relationships fail or tend to flounder. This is because these formulas reveal nothing about a person's sense of identity.

Our relationship with Jesus is no different. Formulaic religion dies, fossilizes.

Jesus never speaks in language formulas. Do you know why? Because every person Jesus interacts with is a unique and distinct identity of whom he is the Creator.

Generative language formation is how Jesus talks to people.

Generative communication seeks to break from these formulas for the sake of allowing one's most authentic self to truly connect with the authentic self of another, creating a new conversation every time you talk and interact.

If we are going to truly abide in Jesus—if we are going to thrive in the life we have been given—it is vital that we seek to be generative in our conversations and interactions with him.

It is so easy to fall into formulaic communication in our prayer life. We go through the motions, ritualize our interactions with Jesus, and fall into familiar patterns for the sake of ease and comfort—or even worse, we use formulas, attempting to impress others or control God.

But Jesus will never come to you in a formula. He respects and loves you too much to talk to you that way. Instead, he'll be generative in how he talks to you—his words are able to create and resurrect life within you.

As we move forward, leaning into this generative way of connecting with Jesus is vital for us to discover who we really are in him and what he has planned for our lives.

> What sorts of religious and prayer formulas do you notice in your own or other people's interactions with God? What do you think some of the goals of these formulaic interactions are?

Attention

Slowly and intentionally read through the following passage three times. As you do, consider what words, phrases, or ideas God might be highlighting for you. Circle or underline what stands out to you, then answer the questions after the passage.

> And when you come before God, don't turn that into a theatrical production either. All these people making a regular show out of their prayers, hoping for fifteen minutes of fame! Do you think God sits in a box seat?
>
> Here's what I want you to do: Find a quiet, secluded place so you won't be tempted to role-play before God. Just be there as simply and honestly as you can manage. The focus will shift from you to God, and you will begin to sense his grace.
>
> The world is full of so-called prayer warriors who are prayer-ignorant. They're full of formulas and programs and advice, peddling techniques for getting what you want from God. Don't fall for that nonsense. This is your Father you are dealing with, and he knows better than you what you need. With a God like this loving you, you can pray very simply. (Matt. 6:5–8 MSG)

> After reading the passage above, what most stands out to you? What parts are confusing to you? What questions do you have?

The passage above comes smack in the middle of Jesus's most famous sermon, what we know today as the Sermon on the Mount. Taking up three full chapters in Matthew, this sermon was directed to Jesus's followers (see 5:1–2), though we also know there was a crowd present and listening to what Jesus had to say (see 7:28).

In this, we see the presence of two distinct groups: the disciples who sought to live in the new and generative ways of the kingdom of God and "the crowd," who were still very much steeped in the religious and cultural formulas of their day.

It is no wonder, then, that Jesus over and over again challenges the formulaic ways of living in that day, comparing them directly with the new and creative ways he teaches. His continuous refrain of "You have heard it said . . . but I tell you . . ." serves as a thread for the entire sermon, reminding us of the greater context of this continuous, interconnected teaching—that Jesus desires to awaken (or reawaken) within us a way of seeing God, ourselves, and the world that brings about the abundant life we were always meant for.

It is in this context that we see Jesus directly challenge the ways of prayer common to his first-century audience: the way of the hypocrites (Greek: *hupokritēs*), a common term for the actors who often wore masks in traditional Greek plays (Jesus's favorite title for the Jewish religious leaders), and the way of the pagans (*ethnikos*), a general term describing non-Jewish people who had their own religious and cultural systems that sought to control the divine through engaging in rigorous formulaic practices.

The first sought to use religious formulas as a means of strengthening their status and power; the other approached the divine with a vending machine mentality (i.e., you put in your money and punch in the right code, and from heaven drops exactly what you want). Neither represented the connection God desires with those he loves.

Jesus contrasts each of these prayer formulas with something else entirely. Whereas each of these so-called "prayer warriors" offered religious rituals, Jesus describes an intimate relationship—that of a child connecting with a loving parent.

In this, Jesus paints a picture of prayer that is not about looking good or manipulating God into giving us what we want. It breaks free of those dead formulas. God is a person with the ability to dynamically and authentically interact with us far outside our regular formulas. Jesus teaches that prayer is about genuine connection between us and our loving Father.

In this generative space of communication, you can start to uncover an ever-greatening truth about both God's identity (as an infinitely good and loving Father) and the cornerstone of your own identity (as a deeply loved and endlessly seen child of God).

> Jesus, in light of or beyond the passage above, what is the most important thing you want to say to me right now?

> Jesus, why are you saying this to me? What do you want me to understand or see differently about myself, you, or the world?

Awareness

Prayerfully consider the last twenty-four hours—morning, afternoon, and evening—allowing yourself to become aware of Jesus's presence with you throughout the day. Chart out your day below.

	What situations, events, experiences, thoughts, and feelings is Jesus highlighting for me?	What does Jesus want to say to me about what he has highlighted?
MORNING		
AFTERNOON		
EVENING		

Considering what Jesus highlighted for you above, ask him how he was present with you throughout your day. How might he want you to notice him in similar situations in the future?

Annunciation

Ask Jesus the following questions, and write out the first thing he brings to your heart or mind.

Jesus, what aspect of my false identity am I holding on to that you want to highlight for me today?

> Jesus, how does that aspect of my false identity lead me to live from a place of fear? How does it awaken in me the desire to compete, compare, self-protect, and/or self-promote?

Pray the following prayer over yourself, lifting up and releasing to Jesus the aspect of your false self he has revealed to you.

Lord Jesus, as I give this aspect of my false identity to you, cleanse me of that lie and the fear it produces. I give it to you now, Christ Jesus. By the power of your life, death, and resurrection, I leave my burdens at the cross and take up your protection from and silencing of the enemy and all the false things in my life. As you bear this false identity in your own flesh, please exchange it within me for my true identity in you.

Next, ask Jesus the following questions about your true identity, again writing out the first thing he brings to your heart or mind.

> Jesus, in light of that false identity, would you speak back to me the name, or identity, that you call me? What do you want to reveal to me about my true identity today? What do you want to announce over me?

> Jesus, how would understanding this aspect of my true identity produce in me courage rather than fear? How would embracing this truth about who I am allow me to thrive in my life?

Pray the following prayer over yourself, holding in your heart and mind the aspect of your true self that Jesus has revealed to you.

Lord Jesus, when I give you my shame, you give me back honor. When I give you my guilt, you give me back innocence. When I give you my fear, you give me back power and authority. By the power of the cross, I claim the beautiful exchange of identity that you make possible for me. In your beautiful voice, Lord, I embrace the aspect of my true identity that you have made known to me today. Thank you for what you call me.

> Jesus, what one word or phrase do you want to leave me with today about my true identity?

Action

Spend some time in generative conversation with Jesus, using a thoughtless task (sweeping, walking, doing the dishes, etc.) to relax your mind.

Use your time to prayerfully consider (by asking generative questions of Jesus) one or more of the following mysteries:

1. *The mystery of God and his universe.* Every day we can explore the mystery of the universe. Those who have committed their lives to understanding this mystery have said, "We're going to figure it out even if we die trying." And when they figure out one thing, they learn there's much more to know.

   Try to understand more of the mystery of God and his universe today. Start by saying, *God, teach me something about you and your universe that I do not know.*

2. *The mystery of you.* Trust me, you do not know yourself. If you did, you would be doing amazing things. The way you think of yourself is way too small. In Psalm 139, David says, in so many words, "God, search me and know me, and reveal any wicked or offensive way in me, and then lead me in a new way. Lead me in the way of everlasting every day" (see vv. 23–24 AMP).

   Try to understand more of the mystery of you. Start by saying, *God, teach me something about myself that I do not know.*

3. *The mystery of others.* Consider the mystery of other people in your world—your kids, spouse, neighbors, coworkers, people you cross paths with regularly. Try to figure them out. After thirty-six years, I'm still working on the mystery of my wife. I've known her since she was nineteen, and she's a beautiful mystery to me. My children are each a beautiful, though sometimes troubling, mystery to me. I love the journey with them and with my neighbors and many others.

   Try to understand more of the mystery of others. Start by saying, *God, teach me something that I do not know about someone else.*

Take some time to write down what God revealed to you about these mysteries.

Consider making this a regular practice, setting aside space multiple times a week to explore these mysteries in generative conversation with God.

For Discussion or Further Reflection

Where in your life do you most rely on a formulaic communication style? Where in your faith do you most rely on a formulaic communication style?

When reading Matthew 6:5–8, what part of Jesus's teaching around prayer was most encouraging to you? What part was most challenging?

When was a time that you experienced Jesus communicating to you in a generative, nonformulaic way? What stands out to you about that experience?

What would it look like for your own communication toward Jesus to go from formulaic to generative? What is one thing you can do this week to engage Jesus in a more generative way?

SESSION 3

VOCATION FLOWS FROM IDENTITY

In the previous session, I told you about my awkward interaction with a young man in a ride share. Through this story, I highlighted how formulaic communication brings about little in the way of real relational connection, with others or with God.

As our interaction continued on the way to the airport, I sought to break free from the formulaic patterns of our conversation and move us into a generative interaction that would actually reveal something about who I was and who he was.

I asked, "Besides driving folks around, what do you do?"

"I don't do anything except drive folks around," he said.

"Wow," I responded.

He said, "My goal is to be on vacation as much time as I can."

That's noble, isn't it? Sociologists and anthropologists say that the two highest goals of people are to be immortal and permanently joyful. If we could, that's what we would do, isn't it? But isn't that life (immortality and joy) in the kingdom of God right now?

This guy assumed he wasn't going to be immortal, but he was going to try to be permanently happy, so he saved up money and flew to Belize as often as he could.

"What do you do there?" I asked.

"My goal is to open up a barbecue restaurant in Belize."

"That's interesting," I said. "Is that your identity?"

"I don't know. I guess it is."

"Running a restaurant's not an identity; it's a vocation. What is your identity? Who are you?"

"I don't know," he said. "I never really thought about that."

He waited a moment and then said, "I have a nephew who's sixteen, and he doesn't have an identity."

My driver could see the lack of identity in another person but not in himself. Isn't that interesting? (Spoiler alert: this is true for all of us.)

"He doesn't have an identity," he continued. "All he does is sit around and play video games. He has no sense of identity."

I asked again, "What's your identity?"

"I don't know. Where does a person get an identity?"

"Where do you think?"

"Maybe from God?" he said.

"Yes, could be," I said. "That's a possibility."

I was doing my best not to engage in any formulaic language in this conversation. No prefabricated gospel presentation. Just simple, generative conversation focused on this amazing young man and who he truly is to God.

So, rather than just offer to him what I believed, I wanted him to consider for himself: *Does God talk to people? Does God talk to you? Does he say, "This is the identity I have for you"? Is that what God does?*

If his answer to these questions was yes—or even maybe—that would mean some pretty amazing things about God. If God talked to us and told us our identity, we would know what to do with our lives. This is because our identity and being inform our doing—who we are directly informs what God has us here to do (or our vocation).

Simple, right?

Well, the truth is most of us live in the complete opposite way, seeking to find our sense of identity in what we do. This, of course, leads us to all sorts of confusion and misinterpretation about both who we are *and* what we are here to do. In short, living this way does not lead to thriving.

Wanting my driver to really consider where his train of thought was leading him, I asked, "*Does* God give identity?"

I could tell he was thinking, and I had been waiting for this. "What's your identity?" he asked.

When a person in a conversation such as this asks, "What's your identity?" it's good to have an answer. Christians are good at talking about stuff that they don't ever really experience. Sometimes this can be a form of lying.

"Well, my identity is *militant peacemaker*," I said to the driver. (Today I would identify as an *untier of knots*—an example of how God will help us to understand our identity to ever deepening degrees as we continue to grow and mature.)

"Wow," he said.

"I know what vocations enable and empower that identity, and I've known this since I was fourteen. Therefore, my vocation has been with the police department, something involved in militant peacemaking."

For the record, a person's vocation (or vocations) encompasses so much more than what they do to make money. A vocation is a natural outpouring of who God has made us to be. I chose a profession in the range of my identity and found that engaging well in that vocation flowed naturally from that identity.

Conversely, if I had picked a career outside of that identity, I would have been unhappy and frustrated, and I would not have been good at it. Every day, I would know I wasn't good at it and that it was going to be bad. I could go to church and I could pray, but it wouldn't make it better because I was not made to do whatever I was doing outside of my identity.

I told the driver I had been a police officer, then I got promoted a lot, then I got recruited by the government, and then I went overseas. My militant peacemaking started small and kept expanding. Professionally, spiritually, up, up, up.

"You mean I would have an identity that leads to running a restaurant?" my new friend asked.

"Yes, yes, that's it."

"And the restaurant would just be an extension of my identity?"

"Yes. That's right."

"I need to find my identity," he said sincerely. "Maybe I need to go to God and find my identity."

Yes! I thought. I think this would be a worthwhile pursuit for us all.

What do you think it means that your identity informs your vocation (that who you are informs what you were made to do)? In what areas of your life do you feel harmony between your identity and your vocation? In what areas do you feel dissonance between your identity and your vocation?

Attention

Slowly and intentionally read through the following passage three times. As you do, consider what words, phrases, or ideas God might be highlighting for you. Circle or underline what stands out to you, then answer the questions after the passage.

> But God is so rich in mercy, and he loved us so much, that even though we were dead because of our sins, he gave us life when he raised Christ from the dead. (It is only by God's grace that you have been saved!) For he raised us from the dead along with Christ and seated us with him in the heavenly realms because we are united with Christ Jesus. So God can point to us in all future ages as examples of the incredible wealth of his grace and kindness toward us, as shown in all he has done for us who are united with Christ Jesus.
>
> God saved you by his grace when you believed. And you can't take credit for this; it is a gift from God. Salvation is not a reward for the good things we have done, so none of us can boast about it. For we are God's masterpiece. He has created us anew in Christ Jesus, so we can do the good things he planned for us long ago. (Eph. 2:4–10 NLT)

> After reading the passage above, what most stands out to you? What parts are confusing to you? What questions do you have?

The passage above comes from a letter written to a church in an ancient Mediterranean city called Ephesus, in modern day Turkey. The city was large, important, and thought of as the epicenter of Greek religious life.

The man who wrote this letter was an apostle ("sent one") named Paul, whose letters make up most of the New Testament. (We will be exploring many of Paul's writings during our time together.) Paul had an incredible encounter with the risen Jesus that transformed his life and sense of identity.

The first half of his letter is spent laying out for his readers the good news about Jesus and how they—mostly non-Jewish believers—are also given a restored identity in Christ. Paul wants them to understand themselves as God's children, ones planned for adoption into God's family even before their creation (see 1:5).

Paul highlights for his readers that this restored identity has nothing to do with what they have done but instead is rooted in the life, death, and resurrection of Jesus. That means that this core part of our identity—as children of God—is not something that changes. It can't be earned or lost. It is an identity based on and given by God through Jesus.

From this concept, Paul then transitions to the second half of the letter, which unpacks how a new way of living then flows from this restored identity in Christ. We can see the structure of the letter reflected in Ephesians 2:10, which reads, "For we are God's masterpiece. He has created us anew in Christ Jesus, so we can do the good things he planned for us long ago" (NLT).

The verse starts with a declaration about our identity: we are God's *masterpiece* (the Greek word *poiēma*), which likens us to a work of art masterfully designed by God—one he is immensely proud of and whose beauty he is compelled to share with others.

That's you! That is who you are! A unique masterwork of the Creator of the universe.

We then see that from that identity—restored by Jesus—flow the good works that God "planned for us long ago." The implication is that we are uniquely created for specific works, that who we are was designed with a particular vocation in mind.

Understanding this is key to our thriving in this life. This means that if we are to truly thrive, we need to spend some time allowing Jesus to affirm and solidify within us our identity as children of God—the foundation of who we are, from which all vocations flow.

> Jesus, in light of or beyond the passage above, what is the most important thing you want to say to me right now?

> Jesus, why are you saying this to me? What do you want me to understand or see differently about myself, you, or the world?

Awareness

Prayerfully consider the last twenty-four hours—morning, afternoon, and evening—allowing yourself to become aware of Jesus's presence with you throughout the day. Chart out your day below.

	What situations, events, experiences, thoughts, and feelings is Jesus highlighting for me?	What does Jesus want to say to me about what he has highlighted?
MORNING		
AFTERNOON		
EVENING		

Considering what Jesus highlighted for you above, ask him how he was present with you throughout your day. How might he want you to notice him in similar situations in the future?

Annunciation

Ask Jesus the following questions, and write out the first thing he brings to your heart or mind.

Jesus, what aspect of my false identity am I holding on to that you want to highlight for me today?

Jesus, how does that aspect of my false identity lead me to live from a place of fear? How does it awaken in me the desire to compete, compare, self-protect, and/or self-promote?

Pray the following prayer over yourself, lifting up and releasing to Jesus the aspect of your false self he has revealed to you.

Lord Jesus, as I give this aspect of my false identity to you, cleanse me of that lie and the fear it produces. I give it to you now, Christ Jesus. By the power of your life, death, and resurrection, I leave my burdens at the cross and take up your protection from and silencing of the enemy and all the false things in my life. As you bear this false identity in your own flesh, please exchange it within me for my true identity in you.

Next, ask Jesus the following questions about your true identity, again writing out the first thing he brings to your heart or mind.

> Jesus, in light of that false identity, would you speak back to me the name, or identity, that you call me? What do you want to reveal to me about my true identity today? What do you want to announce over me?

> Jesus, how would understanding this aspect of my true identity produce in me courage rather than fear? How would embracing this truth about who I am allow me to thrive in my life?

Pray the following prayer over yourself, holding in your heart and mind the aspect of your true self that Jesus has revealed to you.

Lord Jesus, when I give you my shame, you give me back honor. When I give you my guilt, you give me back innocence. When I give you my fear, you give me back power and authority. By the power of the cross, I claim the beautiful exchange of identity that you make possible for me. In your beautiful voice, Lord, I embrace the aspect of my true identity that you have made known to me today. Thank you for what you call me.

> Jesus, what one word or phrase do you want to leave me with today about my true identity?

Action

Write a love letter from God to yourself, with God expressing and affirming his immense love for you as his child. Prayerfully consider what your Creator and Father would want to say to you about how much he loves you as his child and his masterpiece. Use the following verses to focus your mind and heart on God's love for you.

> How priceless is your unfailing love, O God!
> People take refuge in the shadow of your wings. (Ps. 36:7)

When we were utterly helpless, Christ came at just the right time and died for us sinners. Now, most people would not be willing to die for an upright person, though someone might perhaps be willing to die for a person who is especially good. But God showed his great love for us by sending Christ to die for us while we were still sinners. (Rom. 5:6–8 NLT)

I pray that out of his glorious riches he may strengthen you with power through his Spirit in your inner being, so that Christ may dwell in your hearts through faith. And I pray that you, being rooted and established in love, may have power, together with all the Lord's holy people, to grasp how wide and long and high and deep is the love of Christ, and to know this love that surpasses knowledge—that you may be filled to the measure of all the fullness of God. (Eph. 3:16–19)

See how very much our Father loves us, for he calls us his children, and that is what we are! But the people who belong to this world don't recognize that we are God's children because they don't know him. (1 John 3:1 NLT)

This is how God showed his love for us: God sent his only Son into the world so we might live through him. This is the kind of love we are talking about—not that we once upon a time loved God, but that he loved us and sent his Son as a sacrifice to clear away our sins and the damage they've done to our relationship with God. (1 John 4:9–10 MSG)

For Discussion or Further Reflection

How have you noticed yourself trying to find a sense of identity in what you do? What would it look like to instead let what you do flow from your true identity?

Look at Ephesians 2:4–10. What identity statements stand out to you about who we are in Christ? If you really believed that those things were true of you, how might that change how you live?

In what ways have you interpreted God as something other than a loving Father in your relationship with him? What title would you use to describe that interpretation of God (e.g., God as strict disciplinarian, God as distant force, God as shamer, God as weak, God as apathetic, etc.)?

How might you better embrace the truth about who God is (loving Father) and who you are in light of who he is (loved child)? What core beliefs about yourself, God, or the world hinder you from embracing these truths?

SESSION 4
UNIFIED AND UNIQUE

I'm involved in a small group, not a handpicked group but a random group of people from the church my wife and I attend. The group comprises four couples and three single people. Each week, we focus on listening to God and living in true identity. We remind one another that at the core of our identity, we are God's loved children, created in and restored by Jesus.

This truth unifies us. We are not just a collection of friends, not an assigned arrangement of acquaintances. We are a family, sisters and brothers of a common Father, adopted children becoming more and more like our older Brother Jesus. This shared spiritual heritage is the cornerstone of an identity that leads to our thriving.

We are unified by it. But we are also each unique in our identity. From our firm grounding as God's loved children, each of us is created to express that core identity in distinct ways.

I'll give you an example. One of the women in the group—a strong, sharp twenty-eight-year-old—recognized at a young age a pattern of giving and enacting intentional care for those around her. It is a part of how she, as a child of God, looks like her Father—reflecting his deep generosity and attentive care for each and every one of us. In this, she is expressing her identity as God's loved child in a unique way.

In response to this identity, she leaned in, lived in harmony with it, and allowed God to cultivate the identity he planted within her when she was created. She considered those who needed the most care, which led her to start a refugee-care program in our area. Before long, it became one of the best refugee-care programs in the country.

Because of her expertise, I invited this young woman to join me at a conference in Detroit, which has one of the largest refugee centers in the United States. She spoke about her strategy, and in the audience were people representing President Obama, who was in office at the time.

The "experts" stared at her and asked, "Where have you been? How did you accomplish this?" They wanted to know how she had gained this expertise in refugee care and asked her to speak at their main forum in Houston.

All this from understanding her true identity.

And this was an identity that she realized when she was only five years old. That's how long the idea had been inside her, but she couldn't access it apart from God. It was there, waiting to be discovered.

From our weekly gathering, four new enterprises have emerged—four vocational expressions of the unique identities these individuals have been given by God. We are unified in our work for the kingdom but are each working for the kingdom in slightly different ways.

What I want you to realize is that you, too, are a part of this family—unified with us in Christ. But you are also unique. There are ideas inside your mind, heart, and spirit—ideas that no one has ever thought of before. And the beauty is that these ideas want to come out of you.

I'm talking about whatever it is you know that we don't yet know, whatever it is you are specifically equipped to feel and uniquely gifted to do.

The sad part is that, for most, it's not going to happen, because your false self—your fear, guilt, and shame—will shut down your creative and imaginative true self.

But there's good news! It *can* happen, and it can start today. You could say no to it today as well—you have that freedom. But I hope you won't. I hope you will not dare to say no to what is within you. The world needs what you have. The world needs the real you.

> When was a time that you felt distinctly in your identity, like you were (even if just in a small way) living exactly where you were intended to be? What was that experience like?

Attention

Slowly and intentionally read through the following passage three times. As you do, consider what words, phrases, or ideas God might be highlighting for you. Circle or underline what stands out to you, then answer the questions after the passage.

> There are different kinds of spiritual gifts, but the same Spirit is the source of them all. There are different kinds of service, but we serve the same Lord. God works in different ways, but it is the same God who does the work in all of us.
>
> A spiritual gift is given to each of us so we can help each other. To one person the Spirit gives the ability to give wise advice; to another the same Spirit gives a message of special knowledge. The same Spirit gives great faith to another, and to someone else the one Spirit gives the gift of healing. He gives one person the power to perform miracles, and another the ability to prophesy. He gives someone else the ability to discern whether a message is from the Spirit of God or from another spirit. Still another person is given

the ability to speak in unknown languages, while another is given the ability to interpret what is being said. It is the one and only Spirit who distributes all these gifts. He alone decides which gift each person should have.

The human body has many parts, but the many parts make up one whole body. So it is with the body of Christ. (1 Cor. 12:4–12 NLT)

> After reading the passage above, what most stands out to you? What parts are confusing to you? What questions do you have?

The Corinthian church Paul was writing to was a deeply divided community. Paul repeatedly worked to mend and reunify a family of believers who loved to divide into factions around different teachers, focusing on things like wealth, status, and eloquence. Paul is quick to point out, though, that these teachers are not the focus of our lives in Christ. The focus can only be found in the person of Jesus, who is the head of all believers, leading them all through the Holy Spirit.

In this particular section of the letter, Paul is addressing how the gatherings of the Corinthian church were marked by chaotic and self-promoting behavior, individuals using their gifts to talk over and outdo one another. Paul instead encourages them toward allowing the Spirit to unify them and lead them in sacrificial love—like the love Jesus offers us on the cross.

Paul provides an analogy, comparing the family of believers to a human body and communicating how there can be unity while at the same time diversity within the church. The eye works with the hand, unified in purpose, though unique in skill set. Neither is better than the other, and both need each other to function effectively.

It is in this space that we find ourselves both unified and unique in our identities. We are brought together under Christ, who is the head—the source of leading and decision-making faculties—of the body. He leads the members to work together as each of us is activated to use our unique abilities to enact his will here on earth.

Paul continually reminds the Corinthians that in all of this, love is the ultimate goal. As he writes in the very next chapter,

> If I could speak all the languages of earth and of angels, but didn't love others, I would only be a noisy gong or a clanging cymbal. If I had the gift of prophecy, and if I understood all of God's secret plans and possessed all knowledge, and if I had such faith that I could move mountains, but didn't love others, I would be nothing. If I gave everything I have to the poor and even sacrificed my body, I could boast about it; but if I didn't love others, I would have gained nothing. (1 Cor. 13:1–3 NLT)

Jesus, in light of or beyond the passage above, what is the most important thing you want to say to me right now?

Jesus, why are you saying this to me? What do you want me to understand or see differently about myself, you, or the world?

Awareness

Prayerfully consider the last twenty-four hours—morning, afternoon, and evening—allowing yourself to become aware of Jesus's presence with you throughout the day. Chart out your day below.

	What situations, events, experiences, thoughts, and feelings is Jesus highlighting for me?	What does Jesus want to say to me about what he has highlighted?
MORNING		
AFTERNOON		
EVENING		

Considering what Jesus highlighted for you above, ask him how he was present with you throughout your day. How might he want you to notice him in similar situations in the future?

Annunciation

Ask Jesus the following questions, and write out the first thing he brings to your heart or mind.

Jesus, what aspect of my false identity am I holding on to that you want to highlight for me today?

Jesus, how does that aspect of my false identity lead me to live from a place of fear? How does it awaken in me the desire to compete, compare, self-protect, and/or self-promote?

Pray the following prayer over yourself, lifting up and releasing to Jesus the aspect of your false self he has revealed to you.

> *Lord Jesus, as I give this aspect of my false identity to you, cleanse me of that lie and the fear it produces. I give it to you now, Christ Jesus. By the power of your life, death, and resurrection, I leave my burdens at the cross and take up your protection from and silencing of the enemy and all the false things in my life. As you bear this false identity in your own flesh, please exchange it within me for my true identity in you.*

Next, ask Jesus the following questions about your true identity, again writing out the first thing he brings to your heart or mind.

> Jesus, in light of that false identity, would you speak back to me the name, or identity, that you call me? What do you want to reveal to me about my true identity today? What do you want to announce over me?

> Jesus, how would understanding this aspect of my true identity produce in me courage rather than fear? How would embracing this truth about who I am allow me to thrive in my life?

Pray the following prayer over yourself, holding in your heart and mind the aspect of your true self that Jesus has revealed to you.

Lord Jesus, when I give you my shame, you give me back honor. When I give you my guilt, you give me back innocence. When I give you my fear, you give me back power and authority. By the power of the cross, I claim the beautiful exchange of identity that you make possible for me. In your beautiful voice, Lord, I embrace the aspect of my true identity that you have made known to me today. Thank you for what you call me.

> Jesus, what one word or phrase do you want to leave me with today about my true identity?

Action

Spend some time brainstorming in each of the following areas, then use each circle in the diagram below to write words and phrases that capture the ideas you are brainstorming.

Afterward, spend some time in prayer, asking, *Jesus, how might some of these areas intersect? Considering these areas, how might you be calling me to express your love?* Write what God reveals to you in the center of the diagram, where the three circles intersect.

Gifts, Skills & Expertise: Brainstorm some areas in which you and/or others have noticed your proficiency, capacity, or adeptness. Keep in mind that this doesn't mean you will not need to keep learning and growing in these areas, just that you show a natural aptitude or seem to be spiritually gifted in them.

Need & Story: Brainstorm some areas of need (whether in a personal relationship, in your community, or something going on globally) that particularly capture your attention or break your heart. Also consider if there are any parts of your story that God wants to redeem for the sake of loving others in need.

Passion & Interest: Brainstorm some areas that you are particularly passionate about or interested in. Think of areas that give you energy, that draw you in, that capture and captivate you.

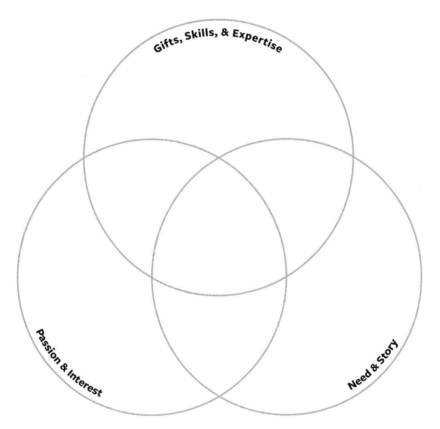

Note: Not everything you write down will intersect with something in another circle. You may be gifted in a certain area and there may be a need, but if you have no passion, it is unlikely that God is calling you to that area. In the same way, you may be passionate about something and there may be a need, but if you are not spiritually gifted in that area, it is perhaps not the right place for you. Finally, you can, of course, be gifted and passionate about something, but if there is no need, it is unlikely that this is where God has you.

For Discussion or Further Reflection

What stands out to you about being both unified and unique in Christ? What do you notice about each of these aspects that helps the family of God function effectively in their identity and vocation?

What aspects of 1 Corinthians 12:4–12 and 13:1–3 stand out to you the most? What is most encouraging to you about the passages? What is most challenging?

Considering what you have uncovered in this session, when was a time that you saw the body of Christ operating as it was intended? When was a time that you noticed something amiss?

Looking at the "Action" activity above, how might God be inviting you to find your unique place in the body of Christ? What steps can you take this week to start exploring this uniqueness?

SESSION 5
THRIVING IN THE NOW

Once, while I was working in a Muslim country, a coworker called me from a neighboring country that was engulfed in civil strife.

He informed me that the previous evening, two men began pounding on his apartment door, demanding entrance. He said, "When I looked through the peephole, I could see the men were dressed as members of an extremist militia in the area. As a newly arrived American worker in the city, I feared for the welfare of myself and my family. I pretended not to be home and the men finally left, but I'm afraid they'll come back tonight. What should I do? Should I flee the city?"

As humans, we can be quite wrong about what we think or conclusions we draw in situations where we're confident that the facts speak for themselves. This mistake occurs most often when we separate our heart from our brain and let our brain go into autopilot. In autopilot, the brain processes everything it sees in the present based on what it has seen and known in the past.

This was the case with my coworker friend. He was an experienced worker in the Middle East, but the suddenness of the event and the resulting fear hindered his ability to be attentive and aware in the new and present scenario.

He defaulted into a reflexive fight-flight-or-freeze mentality, believing that this situation was preventing him from living out his vocation most fully—and perhaps forcing him to leave the place he was so certain God had called him.

It felt like his circumstances were preventing his thriving in the now.

While we talked together, he was able to silence the threatening voices of the enemy and focus his heart and mind on asking God what he wanted him to know and do in the current situation. Rather than fight, flight, or freeze, the Holy Spirit led him into a plan of active engagement for what he was experiencing in the present.

The next night when the men returned, pounding on the door, my friend exited his apartment, locked the door behind him, and walked quickly between them into the street. The men followed him, and once gathered in the street, my friend asked, "What can I do to be of help to you and the other people in this community?"

The men stared at him for several seconds before one of them spoke up. "We know you are new in the neighborhood, and so we came to welcome you and invite you to a dinner with our families."

Rather than fleeing the city in fear and missing an opportunity to impact the neighborhood for Christ, my friend was able to turn his heart to the Father and experience the Father's heart for these Muslim men.

The heart sees each thing anew all the time. However, the brain says, "Nope, we've seen this before. We got hurt. We're not doing it again."

As a result, when God says, "Hey, I have a thing I want you to do in your life; it's going to be incredible," the typical response from our rational mind is, "Nope, too risky." Think about Moses when God first called him to lead the Israelites. His response was, "Find someone else who is a better speaker." Or Gideon, whom God called his "mighty man of valor." His response? "Nope, I'm the least in my family."

But God, in his love and patience, presses us forward. We can feel it down in our heart as we sense, "Let's do this new thing!" Then we dream and have an idea and think, "I can do this!" And then, in our mind we say, "No. No."

Why?

"Because I'm not worthy. I'm filled with shame. I'm afraid. So I cannot do it."

This type of thinking hurts us. If we could live and lead with our heart, what a different life we would experience. Once the heart and mind are brought into balance, with the mind serving the heart, we can live with an unconflicted mind.

Can you imagine living with an unconflicted mind where your heart and mind are always in sync? And even more, your heart and mind are in sync with each other and they're in sync with God? Imagine living like that!

I'm not talking about some religious magic world. I'm not even talking about once you "arrive" at living out your vocation in its fullest form. I'm talking about real life, living now as the person you were always meant to be.

Have you ever stopped to consider that God has something for you today, that you are capable of living the abundant life in your current circumstances?

Yes, God wants to lead you toward a future that more fully expresses what he has you here on earth to do—a vocational reality birthed from your true identity. But that doesn't mean that today is just a holding pattern, getting through the now for the sake of the then.

If I know who I am, and I know how to align my heart and mind in relationship with God, there is really nothing to wait for. As a result, I can do anything in my true identity.

I can really start to thrive, even today.

What do you think holds you back from thriving in the now? Where do you default to the fight-flight-or-freeze mentality? How might God want to invite you into thriving today, in your present reality?

Attention

Slowly and intentionally read through the following passage three times. As you do, consider what words, phrases, or ideas God might be highlighting for you. Circle or underline what stands out to you, then answer the questions after the passage.

> So I say, walk by the Spirit, and you will not gratify the desires of the flesh. For the flesh desires what is contrary to the Spirit, and the Spirit what is contrary to the flesh. They are in conflict with each other, so that you are not to do whatever you want. But if you are led by the Spirit, you are not under the law.
>
> The acts of the flesh are obvious: sexual immorality, impurity and debauchery; idolatry and witchcraft; hatred, discord, jealousy, fits of rage, selfish ambition, dissensions, factions and envy; drunkenness, orgies, and the like. I warn you, as I did before, that those who live like this will not inherit the kingdom of God.
>
> But the fruit of the Spirit is love, joy, peace, forbearance, kindness, goodness, faithfulness, gentleness and self-control. Against such things there is no law. Those who belong to Christ Jesus have crucified the flesh with its passions and desires. Since we live by the Spirit, let us keep in step with the Spirit. (Gal. 5:16–25)

> After reading the passage above, what most stands out to you? What parts are confusing to you? What questions do you have?

At the time of Paul's writing of this letter, the Galatian church had a lot of conflicting teaching going on. There was a whole movement of Jewish Christians from Jerusalem who were teaching that the key to the Christian life was to follow a slew of rules and regulations from the Hebrew Torah (the early books of the Old Testament that contain the Hebrew religious and cultural codes).

Paul makes the case that though this law is ultimately a good thing, it is insufficient in making anyone—whether Jew or otherwise—right with God. For that, we all need to trust in the work of Jesus on the cross, not in our own works or ability to live by some legal code.

The natural question then becomes "Well, does it matter at all how we live? How do we live today?"

Paul's response is "Of course! But things look a little different."

Instead of trying to live a thriving life through our own strength, Jesus empowers us, through his Holy Spirit living inside of us, to embrace a new way of living—one marked by what Paul calls "the fruit of the Spirit." This is contrasted with what Paul calls "the flesh," which are the selfish ways of living that all humanity is predisposed to because of the influence of sin. The idea is that though we are made free in Christ, we are still habituated in these selfish and destructive ways as though they are programmed into our very flesh.

This is what I mean by the mind being out of balance with the heart. Though we have a new heart in Christ, our mind holds on to the residual ways we embraced during our old life.

In this, we as followers of Jesus are given an action step toward thriving in the now. Paul tells us to "walk by the Spirit" (v. 16), to "keep in step with the Spirit" (v. 25). The image here is that Jesus's Spirit walks next to us in life—our eternal companion—and we are to pace ourselves to his steps, rhythm, speed, and path.

When we do, we cultivate the kind of life from which love, joy, peace, patience, kindness, and the like flow naturally. Our role is not to force ourselves into these ways of life as though by a new law but to stay sensitive to what Jesus is doing in and around us in the present—not to strike out ahead or fall behind—and our lives will then overflow with this fruit, leading us to thrive in the now.

> Jesus, in light of or beyond the passage above, what is the most important thing you want to say to me right now?

> Jesus, why are you saying this to me? What do you want me to understand or see differently about myself, you, or the world?

Awareness

Prayerfully consider the last twenty-four hours—morning, afternoon, and evening—allowing yourself to become aware of Jesus's presence with you throughout the day. Chart out your day below.

	What situations, events, experiences, thoughts, and feelings is Jesus highlighting for me?	What does Jesus want to say to me about what he has highlighted?
MORNING		
AFTERNOON		
EVENING		

Considering what Jesus highlighted for you above, ask him how he was present with you throughout your day. How might he want you to notice him in similar situations in the future?

Annunciation

Ask Jesus the following questions, and write out the first thing he brings to your heart or mind.

Jesus, what aspect of my false identity am I holding on to that you want to highlight for me today?

Jesus, how does that aspect of my false identity lead me to live from a place of fear? How does it awaken in me the desire to compete, compare, self-protect, and/or self-promote?

Pray the following prayer over yourself, lifting up and releasing to Jesus the aspect of your false self he has revealed to you.

Lord Jesus, as I give this aspect of my false identity to you, cleanse me of that lie and the fear it produces. I give it to you now, Christ Jesus. By the power of your life, death, and resurrection, I leave my burdens at the cross and take up your protection from and silencing of the enemy and all the false things in my life. As you bear this false identity in your own flesh, please exchange it within me for my true identity in you.

Next, ask Jesus the following questions about your true identity, again writing out the first thing he brings to your heart or mind.

> Jesus, in light of that false identity, would you speak back to me the name, or identity, that you call me? What do you want to reveal to me about my true identity today? What do you want to announce over me?

> Jesus, how would understanding this aspect of my true identity produce in me courage rather than fear? How would embracing this truth about who I am allow me to thrive in my life?

Pray the following prayer over yourself, holding in your heart and mind the aspect of your true self that Jesus has revealed to you.

> *Lord Jesus, when I give you my shame, you give me back honor. When I give you my guilt, you give me back innocence. When I give you my fear, you give me back power and authority. By the power of the cross, I claim the beautiful exchange of identity that you make possible for me. In your beautiful voice, Lord, I embrace the aspect of my true identity that you have made known to me today. Thank you for what you call me.*

> Jesus, what one word or phrase do you want to leave me with today about my true identity?

Action

Go for a walk with Jesus. As you do, ask him in what areas you are out of step with his Spirit. Where are you striking out ahead of him? Where are you falling behind? Ask him to give you one thing that you can do in the next twenty-four hours to act from your true identity. What is one area in which he is inviting you to take up a life of thriving in the now?

Whatever it is you sensed from the Lord, write it down and do it. Remember, obedience is better than sacrifice. Be committed to talk to whomever you're supposed to talk to or go wherever you're supposed to go—whatever it is you sensed from the Lord. Just do it!

Each day, as you're growing and learning, keep asking the Lord these questions: *What do you want me to know today to live into my true identity? And what do you want me to do?* Your being, your true self, will always inform your doing.

For Discussion or Further Reflection

Who is a person you know or have known of who seemed to walk in step with Jesus? How did you notice the fruit of the Spirit manifested in and through their daily life?

Reading Galatians 5:16–25, what is significant to you about the illustration of fruit (something that grows as a natural outpouring of walking with Jesus)? What do you think it means to "keep in step with the Spirit"?

When was a time that you felt Jesus moving in a particular moment of your life? How did you respond to him? What did it look like or what would it have looked like to keep in step with Jesus's Spirit in that moment?

What is one way that Jesus may be inviting you to walk by the Spirit each day this week? How might this practice better help you to tune in to what Jesus is doing in the now of your life?

SESSION 6

WHAT'S IN A NAME?

Throughout Scripture, the concept of identity or naming is very important to God. Consider Jesus's baptism at the initiation of his public ministry.

> In those days Jesus came from Nazareth in Galilee and was baptized by John in the Jordan. And immediately coming up out of the water, He saw the heavens opening, and the Spirit, like a dove, descending upon Him; and a voice came from the heavens: "You are My beloved Son; in You I am well pleased." (Mark 1:9–11 NASB)

Jesus has always possessed this true identity, but here it is spoken publicly by God in order that the community might know and participate in it.

True identity can only be known by truth telling. Truth telling moves us from what is real to what is true. This is important because what is real to me isn't always true, but what is true is always real. I must be willing to acknowledge and confess the real me in order to understand the true me. The real me is telling the truth in any and every situation.

For example, if you ask me if I love God, speaking realistically my answer would have to be "I don't know." Do I want to love him? I think yes. But in reality, I do not know what it means to wholeheartedly love an invisible, formless, ultimate being.

I hope and long to love God; I do. That's the real me.

But God sees the *true* me whom he created. This is what I'm moving toward. I'm moving from the *real* me, the "God have mercy on me, a sinner," to the *true* me, the "you are my untier of knots; let's go live that identity together. Come with me; follow me; give me your burden and take mine. Let's go."

You also have a true you—your God-given name/identity from which your purpose in this life flows. This is where you start to realize how you are a gift to this world—how you are uniquely programmed to live and thrive and serve God and others. In this place, you will find the fullness of your vocation, a state of living where your true identity is most free.

The good news is that the true you is already inside you, germinating and waiting to sprout up when given the chance.

Let's look at the life of King David as an example. At around age fifteen, David had encounters with a lion and a bear, both of which he killed with a slingshot. As a ninth grader, David was able to shepherd his sheep and protect them from both lions and bears with his skill in battle.

From this account, we can surmise what elementary and middle school–aged David was doing with his time. He was learning to shepherd sheep and throw stones with a sling. At middle school age or younger, David was practicing the very skills that would make him one of Israel's greatest warriors and kings.

When young David was anointed king of Israel by the prophet Samuel, he became Saul's musician and one of his armor bearers (see 1 Sam.

16). We can guess that this wasn't his first foray into music and poetry. As a young boy he must have been exercising the very thing that would bring him closer and closer to who he was destined to be—and to his writing of most of the biblical psalms.

And here's the amazing thing: when David was anointed king, he did not become king for many years (probably close to two decades). Yet the Hebrew Scripture says that on the day of David's anointing, "The Spirit of the LORD rushed upon David from that day forward" (1 Sam. 16:13 ESV).

Did you catch when the Holy Spirit left David? Never.

Do you know why the Holy Spirit rushed upon him when he was anointed king? Because that was David's identity. That's the true David. The real David can kill lions and write poetry, but only the *true* David is a shepherd-poet-warrior-king filled with the Spirit of God.

Was he a king yet? No, he wasn't yet officially a king. Even so, he was truly a king at that time and forever. The point is, David's true identity in the kingdom of God, from the day God knit him together in his mother's womb, was shepherd-poet-warrior-king.

In the same way, the real you can accomplish things. But the true you—empowered by the Holy Spirit—can do things far beyond what you ever could imagine.

Wherever you find yourself at today, you can go higher, understand your identity more deeply, live out your vocation more fully.

If you sense from God that you are a healer of nations and you're currently working at a gas station, you should start pursuing the skills now to become someone who heals and who brings healing on a large scale.

He's always communicating to the unique, worthy, and loved true you.

Can you hear him? What name does he want to give you?

Prayerfully consider what aspects of your identity God might be highlighting in you today. How might you start leaning into those aspects of your identity now, even if they won't be fully realized until sometime in the future?

Attention

Slowly and intentionally read through the following passage three times. As you do, consider what words, phrases, or ideas God might be highlighting for you. Circle or underline what stands out to you, then answer the questions after the passage.

> The angel of the LORD came and sat down under the oak in Ophrah that belonged to Joash the Abiezrite, where his son Gideon was threshing wheat in a winepress to keep it from the Midianites. When the angel of the LORD appeared to Gideon, he said, "The LORD is with you, mighty warrior."
> "Pardon me, my lord," Gideon replied, "but if the LORD is with us, why has all this happened to us? Where are all his wonders that our ancestors told us about when they said, 'Did not the LORD bring us up out of Egypt?' But now the LORD has abandoned us and given us into the hand of Midian."
> The LORD turned to him and said, "Go in the strength you have and save Israel out of Midian's hand. Am I not sending you?"
> "Pardon me, my lord," Gideon replied, "but how can I save Israel? My clan is the weakest in Manasseh, and I am the least in my family."
> The LORD answered, "I will be with you, and you will strike down all the Midianites, leaving none alive." (Judg. 6:11–16)

> After reading the passage above, what most stands out to you? What parts are confusing to you? What questions do you have?

The book of Judges chronicles the early centuries of Israel living in the land God promised to them after wandering in the wilderness for forty years (and coming out of centuries of slavery in Egypt). The book tells the story of the people of Israel failing to live in their identity as God's chosen people—set apart from the evil ways of the rest of the world and through which "all nations on earth will be blessed" (Gen. 22:18).

Over and over again Israel gets pulled into the same cycle of living outside their God-given identity, being handed over to the evil people they are emulating, being oppressed by those people, calling out to God, and God sending a deliverer (or "judge") to rescue Israel and restore them to true identity in God. Unfortunately, this cycle also includes the Israelites embracing false identities and falling back into the evil ways of humanity time and time again.

Gideon's story comes in the early middle of the book of Judges, where we find a man hiding from the Midianites for fear that they are going to take his harvest. We see that Gideon no longer understands who God truly is, believing God to have left Israel entirely (see 6:13). Furthermore, like most of Israel at this point, Gideon has fully bought into his false identity, seeing himself and his whole clan as weak (see v. 15).

God, however, gives Gideon a different name of "mighty warrior" (v. 12). This is before Gideon has ever won a battle, while he is actively hiding out for fear of those he is supposed to conquer. God helps Gideon to see that his might and the might of God's people will never be found in their own strength or impressiveness but in their reliance on and trust in a good God who will never leave them fully.

Gideon, accompanied by only three hundred men, does eventually embrace his identity. He trusts in God, and the Midianites are defeated through a clever plan, not through numbers or military might.

Sadly, Gideon soon forgets how the Lord is the source of his true identity and might. He leads the people of Israel back into violence, evil, and idolatry.

From there, the judges of Israel only get worse. The book is a tragedy that outlines the hopelessness of all people who seek to live on their own without God, and it provides the backstory of God's anointing of David and his family line to serve as the kings of Israel.

It is also from this family line that Jesus is born and becomes the King of Kings, the ultimate hope of all humanity, who restores us all back to our God-given identities.

> Jesus, in light of or beyond the passage above, what is the most important thing you want to say to me right now?

> Jesus, why are you saying this to me? What do you want me to understand or see differently about myself, you, or the world?

Awareness

Prayerfully consider the last twenty-four hours—morning, afternoon, and evening—allowing yourself to become aware of Jesus's presence with you throughout the day. Chart out your day below.

	What situations, events, experiences, thoughts, and feelings is Jesus highlighting for me?	What does Jesus want to say to me about what he has highlighted?
MORNING		
AFTERNOON		
EVENING		

Considering what Jesus highlighted for you above, ask him how he was present with you throughout your day. How might he want you to notice him in similar situations in the future?

Annunciation

Ask Jesus the following questions, and write out the first thing he brings to your heart or mind.

Jesus, what aspect of my false identity am I holding on to that you want to highlight for me today?

Jesus, how does that aspect of my false identity lead me to live from a place of fear? How does it awaken in me the desire to compete, compare, self-protect, and/or self-promote?

Pray the following prayer over yourself, lifting up and releasing to Jesus the aspect of your false self he has revealed to you.

Lord Jesus, as I give this aspect of my false identity to you, cleanse me of that lie and the fear it produces. I give it to you now, Christ Jesus. By the power of your life, death, and resurrection, I leave my burdens at the cross and take up your protection from and silencing of the enemy and all the false things in my life. As you bear this false identity in your own flesh, please exchange it within me for my true identity in you.

Next, ask Jesus the following questions about your true identity, again writing out the first thing he brings to your heart or mind.

> Jesus, in light of that false identity, would you speak back to me the name, or identity, that you call me? What do you want to reveal to me about my true identity today? What do you want to announce over me?

> Jesus, how would understanding this aspect of my true identity produce in me courage rather than fear? How would embracing this truth about who I am allow me to thrive in my life?

Pray the following prayer over yourself, holding in your heart and mind the aspect of your true self that Jesus has revealed to you.

Lord Jesus, when I give you my shame, you give me back honor. When I give you my guilt, you give me back innocence. When I give you my fear, you give me back power and authority. By the power of the cross, I claim the beautiful exchange of identity that you make possible for me. In your beautiful voice, Lord, I embrace the aspect of my true identity that you have made known to me today. Thank you for what you call me.

> Jesus, what one word or phrase do you want to leave me with today about my true identity?

Action

Spend some time in prayer, asking God to reveal to you some aspect of your true identity by giving you a name. Start by praying the following prayer:

Lord, cleanse me of the aspects of my false identity that I am holding on to. I give them to you, Jesus, to bear in your own flesh, and I take up in exchange the true identity you declare over me.

Father, as I give you these aspects of my false identity, I pray that you would make me safe within your protection and your silencing of the enemy and all the false things in my life. In your beautiful and loving voice, Lord, would you speak over me the true name that you call me?

On the name tag below, write down the name that God reveals to you. It can be a word, a collection of words, a phrase, or an actual name with a meaning. Once you've done that, take a picture of the name tag and save the photo file where you can refer to it often. Or write it out on a sticky note and place it somewhere you will regularly see it. Consider somewhere like next to your toothbrush or on the dashboard of your car. Then, when you are brushing your teeth or driving on your commute, ask, *God, how do you want me to live in and from that name today?*

For Discussion or Further Reflection

What areas of your God-given identity are most difficult for you to embrace in the now? What might change if you were able to fully embrace this aspect of your identity in the present?

When reading the story of Gideon, what stands out to you most? How can understanding ourselves in our truest identity lead us forward in living out our calling, even today?

Considering the name God gave you in the "Action" activity above, in what ways are you living in harmony with that name? In what ways are you living out of harmony?

In what ways might God be calling you to more fully embrace your name this week? How might living as your true self now help lead you toward living more fully in your vocation in the future?

SESSION 7

THE FALSE SELF

Earlier I shared about the rather special small group my wife and I are a part of at our church. Over the years God has called our members to a number of unique ministries and vocations. One such member shared an idea about opening a fitness center for marginalized communities in our city. It's a brilliant concept.

"How did you come up with that idea?" I asked.

He said, "I've kind of just known to do it."

"How long have you known?"

"Ten years."

I marveled at the answer. What an incredible idea that all this time was not seeing the light of day. Why? The problem was that this man allowed so much of his false self to lead and guide his life. When he thought about pursuing this idea, a tremendous amount of fear, guilt, and shame rose to the surface.

Ten years.

The idea had been buried down inside of him, beneath a deep sense of unworthiness and inadequacy. The idea could not be realized because he didn't know his true identity and thus didn't know how to give birth to the idea.

How often is this true for each of us?

What ideas, dreams, and callings do you have that are not being realized because they are buried beneath heavy layers of false beliefs about yourself, about God, and about others?

When we allow these false narratives to rule in our mind and heart, they cut the legs from under us; they steal our courage, preventing us from pursuing our God-given vocations. But the Bible narrative is all about creativity bursting forth from the true self, the true you. This is what it means to thrive.

The primary obstacles to being led by God to live in our truest self are fear, shame, and guilt. Fear (belief that God is not capable), shame (belief that we are unworthy, not good enough), and guilt (belief that our sin has the final word) are all aspects of our false identity that need to be confessed.

Everything from "I look at pornography" to "I eat too much," "I drink too much," "I don't do this," "I need to do that," and so on makes us feel one of three things: fear, guilt, or shame.

Fear, guilt, and shame are false identities. It won't matter how many accountability groups you go to, podcasts you listen to, or books you read, if you live in fear, you are still going to try to control things in order to cope with your anxiety. Your identity is fear.

If your identity is based on guilt, you will struggle with a negative sense of self-worth and self-esteem. Guilt leads to an identity of unworthiness.

If you embrace an identity of unworthiness, you will act like an unworthy person. It doesn't matter where you are or whom you are with. You'll still act to prove your worth and value. You'll set up all the chairs, or you'll be the first one at church every week.

Why? Because you're overflowing with joy?

No, because you're trying to prove that you are worthy.

Only God makes you worthy. Only God removes shame and replaces it with value. On the cross, Jesus canceled all guilt and its resulting shame. Your works cannot accomplish this. Receive the free gift of God.

The longer you succumb to the temptation of the enemy to prove your worth, the deeper this deception is reinforced. You are a slave in bondage to fear, guilt, and shame.

Unfortunately, where most of us live is in the "false me." I feel unworthy because I accept the lie that I am unworthy. "I am unworthy" is an identity statement, and when I live my life according to this identity, I spend all my time trying to earn worthiness, all the while suspecting that I cannot. This sort of life is painful. This is me living from the false self.

When a person says to me, "I'm addicted to pornography," I say, "That's not who you are. You are describing an action. That's not an identity. What is your identity?" A person who is addicted to pornography has a false identity that permits them to be addicted to pornography. What's that false identity?

Generally, I find they embrace the name *unworthy*.

Unworthy people hide in secret rooms in places where they can't be rejected. Shame-filled people waste hours alone in solitude. Even if it is not physical solitude, they find ways to never let anyone see all of who they are. They live in these dark, isolated "places" because they believe no one wants to be with them, and that feels true to them.

That is not real, and it's definitely not true. But we interact with people as if their false identity is real and true.

Perhaps my neighbor is hostile toward me, so I return their hostility. In doing so, I verify and validate that false identity. But why does my neighbor hate me? Perhaps they're experiencing fear, guilt, and shame, which they project onto me. Then I self-protect and self-promote because my neighbor's violence makes me feel powerless and unworthy and fearful. So I project back onto them.

And so goes the conflict, a repetitive cycle of people living out of their false selves, acting out toward one another in ways that create more and more pain, wounds, and false beliefs within each other.

It is so important that we break this cycle.

> Where in your life do you see fear, guilt, and/or shame hold you back from embracing your true identity? What sort of false names have you embraced over the years (e.g., unworthy, weak, unlovable, etc.)?

Attention

Slowly and intentionally read through the following passage three times. As you do, consider what words, phrases, or ideas God might be highlighting for you. Circle or underline what stands out to you, then answer the questions after the passage.

> In the spring of the year, when kings normally go out to war, David sent Joab and the Israelite army to fight the Ammonites. They destroyed the Ammonite army and laid siege to the city of Rabbah. However, David stayed behind in Jerusalem.
>
> Late one afternoon, after his midday rest, David got out of bed and was walking on the roof of the palace. As he looked out over the city, he noticed a woman of unusual beauty taking a bath. He sent someone to find out who she was, and he was told, "She is Bathsheba, the daughter of Eliam and the wife of Uriah the Hittite." Then David sent messengers to get her; and when she came to the palace, he slept with her. She had

just completed the purification rites after having her menstrual period. Then she returned home. Later, when Bathsheba discovered that she was pregnant, she sent David a message, saying, "I'm pregnant." (2 Sam. 11:1–5 NLT)

> After reading the passage above, what most stands out to you? What parts are confusing to you? What questions do you have?

In the previous session we looked at how King David was given the identity of shepherd-poet-warrior-king, an identity which he possessed long before he was ever king of Israel.

Here we find David in a very different circumstance. Now as the king of Israel for decades, David has had much success as God's anointed ruler. God has promised to raise up one of David's descendants to rule forever as King with God as his Father and set up a "house" in which God will dwell for eternity (see 2 Sam. 7). (The "King" alluded to here is of course Jesus, and the "house" in which God will dwell is the family of believers, the church.)

In the meantime, David has united the people of Israel and expanded the kingdom to unprecedented size and power in the region. This is where David's story takes a turn. We are told that, coming off one of his greatest military victories, David didn't go to war with his army but stayed behind in Jerusalem "when kings normally go out to war."

Remember David's identity? He is God's shepherd-poet-warrior-king.

He is neglecting to live in his God-given identity. As to why he makes this decision, we are not told, but it isn't long before David is living out a false identity, one that ultimately leads him and his family down a path of destruction.

This—the forcible taking of another man's wife—is the first of many dominoes to fall and begins the shift of David's story from unprecedented success to abysmal failure.

This part of David's life provides us a cautionary tale of how living outside of our true identities—which is really living without trust in God—can lead not only to the ruin of our own lives but to the ruin of generations to come.

Thankfully, God brought about—from the line of David—the King of Kings to silence the lies of the false self within us and to bring our true self back to life. That means that in Jesus we are able to live as our truest selves, by the names and identities we have been given from God.

> Jesus, in light of or beyond the passage above, what is the most important thing you want to say to me right now?

> Jesus, why are you saying this to me? What do you want me to understand or see differently about myself, you, or the world?

Awareness

Prayerfully consider the last twenty-four hours—morning, afternoon, and evening—allowing yourself to become aware of Jesus's presence with you throughout the day. Chart out your day below.

	What situations, events, experiences, thoughts, and feelings is Jesus highlighting for me?	What does Jesus want to say to me about what he has highlighted?
MORNING		
AFTERNOON		
EVENING		

Considering what Jesus highlighted for you above, ask him how he was present with you throughout your day. How might he want you to notice him in similar situations in the future?

Annunciation

Ask Jesus the following questions, and write out the first thing he brings to your heart or mind.

Jesus, what aspect of my false identity am I holding on to that you want to highlight for me today?

Jesus, how does that aspect of my false identity lead me to live from a place of fear? How does it awaken in me the desire to compete, compare, self-protect, and/or self-promote?

Pray the following prayer over yourself, lifting up and releasing to Jesus the aspect of your false self he has revealed to you.

Lord Jesus, as I give this aspect of my false identity to you, cleanse me of that lie and the fear it produces. I give it to you now, Christ Jesus. By the power of your life, death, and resurrection, I leave my burdens at the cross and take up your protection from and silencing of the enemy and all the false things in my life. As you bear this false identity in your own flesh, please exchange it within me for my true identity in you.

Next, ask Jesus the following questions about your true identity, again writing out the first thing he brings to your heart or mind.

> Jesus, in light of that false identity, would you speak back to me the name, or identity, that you call me? What do you want to reveal to me about my true identity today? What do you want to announce over me?

> Jesus, how would understanding this aspect of my true identity produce in me courage rather than fear? How would embracing this truth about who I am allow me to thrive in my life?

Pray the following prayer over yourself, holding in your heart and mind the aspect of your true self that Jesus has revealed to you.

Lord Jesus, when I give you my shame, you give me back honor. When I give you my guilt, you give me back innocence. When I give you my fear, you give me back power and authority. By the power of the cross, I claim the beautiful exchange of identity that you make possible for me. In your beautiful voice, Lord, I embrace the aspect of my true identity that you have made known to me today. Thank you for what you call me.

> Jesus, what one word or phrase do you want to leave me with today about my true identity?

Action

You have spent the last several sessions considering the aspects of your false identity in the "Annunciation" section of each session. Given this practice, what theme or root aspect of your false identity do you notice across the sessions? Maybe it is a sense of unworthiness, a deep shame, the feeling that you are unlovable, believing you are inadequate, sensing you will never be enough, or something else.

Consider all this with Jesus, walking with him through each of the following questions, writing down what first comes to mind.

Note: This prayer activity can bring up difficult and, at times, traumatic memories. Give yourself permission to take your time and stop if needed. If ever necessary, reach out to a counselor, pastor, or trusted friend to process this prayer time in community.

Lord Jesus, in your name I pray for your protection over me from the lies and the Liar. What theme or root aspect of my false identity do you want me to focus on during this prayer time?

Lord, when did I first begin to feel or believe this aspect of my false identity? Give me a specific memory about this. What about that time caused me to embrace this false identity?

Lord Jesus, I know that you are always present with me and were present with me during this memory. Will you show me where you were and what you were doing then?

Lord, what do you want to say to me or show me about this memory? Where might you want to offer me your divine healing? What do you want to say to me or show me about this theme or root aspect of my false identity?

Lord Jesus, in your name I reject the lie of this root aspect of my false identity. Where do you want to heal me in response to this memory and lie? What truth, verse, or gift do you want me to embrace?

Lord Jesus, thank you for healing me from this root aspect of my false self. In your name I ask that you would seal this theme or root aspect of my false identity away from me and my inner sense of self. Instead, help me to take up and seal within me the truth that you have given me, and help me to live in my true restored identity in you. Amen.

For Discussion or Further Reflection

How have you seen fear, guilt, and shame hold others back from living in their true identity? Which of these aspects is most challenging for you?

When hearing the story of David's failure, what stands out to you most? What do you personally notice most about identity and vocation from this story?

Where in your life have you seen living from a false sense of self lead to pain or destruction? How have you seen living from your truest self lead to moments of thriving?

Where might Jesus be inviting you out of your false identity today? What aspect of your true self might he want you to live from instead?

SESSION 8

CONFESSION: THE START OF TRANSFORMATION

As a police officer, when I arrested somebody, I would bring them in and ask for a *confession*. I didn't ask them for an apology. We teach confession as though it were just saying, "I'm sorry, I'm sorry, I'm sorry." If a police officer hands you a pen and paper and says, "Write the truth about what happened," and you write, "I'm sorry, I'm sorry, I'm sorry," it resolves nothing.

In the church, many of us grew up thinking confession was just telling everyone and God that we're sorry about stuff. But "I'm sorry" doesn't lead to transformation—it doesn't lead to a life of thriving.

Confession is telling God the truth—what you've done, what you feel, and what you really believe—about him, yourself, and others. It is laying out before God exactly where you're at in a given moment, even if you know what you are feeling isn't fully rooted in reality. This isn't for God's sake, of course, but for us—to help us see where we are embracing lies and where God wants to speak truth into our hearts.

It's a powerful act that has been practiced in the church for centuries. God loves honest confession.

Confession is always the beginning of genuine transformation. If you don't tell God your truth, how can he enlighten your reality with his truth?

If I say to God, "I think you let me down every day, and I'm afraid to take a new job because I'm afraid you won't show up," he will always work with that. Always. He will respond to truth. Jesus says, "For if you embrace the truth, it will release true freedom into your lives" (John 8:32 TPT).

Truth always sets you free. Hiding the truth always makes you a slave. If you will not tell the truth, you're in bondage to the lie, the deception, and the rationalization. Don't apologize for your perceived reality; tell the truth about it. That's confession.

Remorse is not repentance.

Confession activates repentance. Repentance is changing the way you think, turning and going a new way. God tells you the truth about who he really is, who you really are, and who your neighbor really is.

God's truth empowers you to believe in a new way, which leads to thinking in a new way, which leads to acting in a new way. He awakens your true identity for the sake of changing your thinking, feeling, and acting—to lead you into a life of thriving. This is transformation.

Confession, repentance, transformation.

We practice confession and repentance all the time. Every time I feel intimidated by a situation, I say, "God, let me tell you how I feel right now." God already knows how I feel and what I really believe. I'm not faking him out. I just say, "Lord, I feel really intimidated. I feel fearful right now. I feel powerless with this person. That's how I feel."

That's confession.

Notice I'm not saying, "Lord, I'm so sorry for feeling afraid; please take the fear away."

God doesn't want to remove the fear; he wants to transform it. Acknowledging the truth about your fear opens the way for repentance and for your truth (fear) to be transformed by God's truth. Then you have authority over the fear rather than the fear controlling you. That is called freedom.

Several years ago, a friend of mine called to tell me that her husband of ten years had suddenly begun staying out late at night, drinking in a local bar. She questioned him about his abrupt, very-out-of-character behavior to which he responded with shrugs and silence.

After several requests, the husband agreed to meet with me. Rather than questioning him about his behavior, I asked him to simply tell God the truth about why he was resisting going home after work.

"I'm afraid that my wife is going to leave me," he confessed, "so I'm preparing myself for the rejection."

He elaborated: "When I was young, my dad was a construction worker and my mom was a school secretary. My mom worked hard in night school and earned a master's degree in education. The week after her graduation, she abandoned the family to pursue a new life with more 'educated' people. My fear is that my wife, who is about to finish her graduate degree, is going to leave me behind because I'm just a high school–educated construction worker like my dad."

The husband literally shook with fear at the prospect of losing the woman he loved. His wife had no intention of leaving him, but his fear was driving him to bring about the separation himself. His fear also prevented him from sharing with his wife his deep sense of unworthiness.

It wasn't until he confessed to God his wrong belief about himself and his wife that he was able to hear God call him an "honorable and worthy son." Then, as an honorable and worthy son, he had the courage to confess his fears to his wife and turn and go a new direction. They laughed and cried together as God's truth brought them into deeper intimacy and understanding with one another.

God's response to true confession is always grace and mercy.

He might whisper, "Beautiful. Let's work with that. No one has authority over you. No one ever has or ever will. I brought you into this situation because this is what I want to accomplish with you. This person needs you. They're hurt. They need you."

Boom! From this confession God has infused us with the power of our true identity, enabling us to repent. Turn around from that old way of thinking—from that aspect of your false self—and go the new way God has offered you, embracing your truest identity.

That's confession and repentance. When you live in continuous confession and repentance, your life is transformed in every area: professionally, spiritually, physically.

In every way, you begin to thrive.

> Where do you struggle to be honest with God? How might honest confession before God help begin the transformation process in those areas?

Attention

Slowly and intentionally read through the following passage three times. As you do, consider what words, phrases, or ideas God might be highlighting for you. Circle or underline what stands out to you, then answer the questions after the passage.

> This is the message we have heard from him and declare to you: God is light; in him there is no darkness at all. If we claim to have fellowship with him and yet walk in the darkness, we lie and do not live out the truth. But if we walk in the light, as he is in the light, we have fellowship with one another, and the blood of Jesus, his Son, purifies us from all sin.
>
> If we claim to be without sin, we deceive ourselves and the truth is not in us. If we confess our sins, he is faithful and just and will forgive us our sins and purify us from all unrighteousness. If we claim we have not sinned, we make him out to be a liar and his word is not in us. (1 John 1:5–10)

After reading the passage above, what most stands out to you? What parts are confusing to you? What questions do you have?

The books known as 1, 2, and 3 John are interconnected writings, almost certainly written by the same author as the Gospel of John, who is referred to as "the one whom Jesus loved" (see John 13:23). We know this because of the literary style, which all of these books share.

The book of 1 John reads more like a sermon than a letter and is written to a specific group of churches that are having problems with false teachers who are denying Jesus. John—a disciple of Jesus during his earthly ministry—identifies himself as an eyewitness to Jesus and to the message John is about to preach, adding instant credibility to what he is writing and setting himself apart from these false teachers, who presumably hadn't been eyewitnesses.

In this passage, he identifies God as light—the first of two main themes in his sermon, the other being "God is love" (1 John 4:8). Though it can be tempting to think of John's challenge to "walk in the light, as he is in the light" as a call to live a perfect life like Jesus, without sin, that doesn't seem to be what John is getting at here.

Instead, he says right away, "If we claim to be without sin, we deceive ourselves and the truth is not in us." In this passage, we find a clue as to what it means to be in the light of God—in essence, to be in the truth. That is why coming out of this passage, John writes, "If we confess our sins, he is faithful and just and will forgive us our sins and purify us from all unrighteousness."

John is sharing with his readers how Jesus has flipped transformation on its head. Conventional wisdom might say, "Show me you can live differently, and then I will forgive you." But Jesus actually shows us that the only way to live differently is to receive his forgiveness.

So, when we walk in honest confession—exposing all the hidden corners and crevices of our heart to God's purifying light—we allow the forgiveness of Jesus to take hold in the places that we are most ashamed and fearful of.

This forgiveness then enables us to see these areas as part of the false self and allows us to turn away from those lies. In this way, we are transformed by Jesus as he reestablishes our true identity within us, from which the life we were created for can flow.

So, when we are tempted to hide in the darkness—believing that if we can fix things on our own first, we will then be accepted by God—Jesus instead calls us in his love and grace to continually come into the light of truth through confession, to receive his forgiveness and then the transformation that flows from it.

> Jesus, in light of or beyond the passage above, what is the most important thing you want to say to me right now?

> Jesus, why are you saying this to me? What do you want me to understand or see differently about myself, you, or the world?

Awareness

Prayerfully consider the last twenty-four hours—morning, afternoon, and evening—allowing yourself to become aware of Jesus's presence with you throughout the day. Chart out your day below.

	What situations, events, experiences, thoughts, and feelings is Jesus highlighting for me?	What does Jesus want to say to me about what he has highlighted?
MORNING		
AFTERNOON		
EVENING		

Considering what Jesus highlighted for you above, ask him how he was present with you throughout your day. How might he want you to notice him in similar situations in the future?

Annunciation

Ask Jesus the following questions, and write out the first thing he brings to your heart or mind.

Jesus, what aspect of my false identity am I holding on to that you want to highlight for me today?

Jesus, how does that aspect of my false identity lead me to live from a place of fear? How does it awaken in me the desire to compete, compare, self-protect, and/or self-promote?

Pray the following prayer over yourself, lifting up and releasing to Jesus the aspect of your false self he has revealed to you.

Lord Jesus, as I give this aspect of my false identity to you, cleanse me of that lie and the fear it produces. I give it to you now, Christ Jesus. By the power of your life, death, and resurrection, I leave my burdens at the cross and take up your protection from and silencing of the enemy and all the false things in my life. As you bear this false identity in your own flesh, please exchange it within me for my true identity in you.

Next, ask Jesus the following questions about your true identity, again writing out the first thing he brings to your heart or mind.

> Jesus, in light of that false identity, would you speak back to me the name, or identity, that you call me? What do you want to reveal to me about my true identity today? What do you want to announce over me?

> Jesus, how would understanding this aspect of my true identity produce in me courage rather than fear? How would embracing this truth about who I am allow me to thrive in my life?

Pray the following prayer over yourself, holding in your heart and mind the aspect of your true self that Jesus has revealed to you.

Lord Jesus, when I give you my shame, you give me back honor. When I give you my guilt, you give me back innocence. When I give you my fear, you give me back power and authority. By the power of the cross, I claim the beautiful exchange of identity that you make possible for me. In your beautiful voice, Lord, I embrace the aspect of my true identity that you have made known to me today. Thank you for what you call me.

> Jesus, what one word or phrase do you want to leave me with today about my true identity?

Action

In the space provided, spend some time going through a practice of confession with God, centering yourself on the following passage:

> If we confess our sins, he is faithful and just and will forgive us our sins and purify us from all unrighteousness. (1 John 1:9)

Father God, thank you for loving and forgiving me by the power of your Son, Jesus Christ. Thank you for purifying me from my unrighteous acts, words, thoughts, and beliefs. I confess that I have been sinful—that I have missed the mark of who you have made me to be and what you have for me to do here on earth.

Father God, bring to mind anything and everything that would be good for me to confess—whether I've recognized it as sin or not—all the while reminding me that my shame has been put to death with Jesus on the cross.

~ ~ ~

*Father, what **actions** do I need to tell you the truth about today?*

Thank you for your forgiveness, Father.

*Father, what **thoughts** do I need to tell you the truth about today?*

Thank you for your forgiveness, Father.

*Father, what **words** do I need to tell you the truth about today?*

Thank you for your forgiveness, Father.

> *Father, what **beliefs**—about you, myself, or others—do I need to tell you the truth about today?*

Thank you for your forgiveness, Father.

> *Father, what does **repentance** look like today? (What is one way I can turn from my false identity and live from my true self today?)*

Father, thank you for purifying me in the name of your Son, Jesus Christ, and by the power of his life, death, and resurrection. Amen.

There are more of these confession pages in the back of this journal. Consider building a regular rhythm of confession, using the pages until you have internalized the rhythm.

For Discussion or Further Reflection

What do you think it means that the start of transformation is always honest confession? What do you think makes honest confession so powerful?

When reading 1 John 1:5–10, how is the metaphor "God is light" helpful to your understanding of honest confession? What do you think John means when he writes the phrase "walk in the darkness"?

What do you think holds you back from honestly confessing to God? What false beliefs might be hindering you from telling God the truth?

Where in your life do you desire to see God's transformation of you in Jesus Christ? How might a regular rhythm of confession help to open you to this transformation?

SESSION 9

LEARNING TO *HEAR*

As we move forward into the thriving that God has for each of us, it's important to understand what it means to really *hear* God. The word for *hear* in Hebrew is *sh'ma*, which is also the title of one of Judaism's most sacred prayers, found in Deuteronomy 6:4–9. The prayer begins:

> Hear [*sh'ma*], O Israel: The Lord our God, the Lord is one. Love the Lord your God with all your heart and with all your soul and with all your strength. (vv. 4–5)

It is famously referenced by Jesus when asked about the greatest commandment (see Matt. 22:36–40). The word *sh'ma* in Deuteronomy 6:4 is generally translated "hear," and this is correct.

However, the word *sh'ma* is also often translated into the English word *obey*, which can cause the Hebraic idea of listening to God to be reduced to the idea of following a list of codified rules and regulations apart from a living, dialogical relationship with the God who speaks.

There is no Hebrew word meaning "obey"; neither is there an English word for *sh'ma*. While this Hebrew verb is often translated as "hear," it means much more than just hearing or listening but rather "to hear and respond appropriately."

When the Hebrew Scriptures say that someone "heard" God, it means that they heard him and then acted on what they heard. When the Hebrew Scriptures say that God "heard" the people, it means that he heard them and then acted on what he heard.

So when we talk about obeying God, let's think beyond rule following to really hearing God and then responding appropriately to what we hear.

Take, for example, Moses and his interaction with God through the burning bush. In this dialogical interchange, which is initiated by God, between the human and the divine, God speaks the truth of God's identity—I AM WHO I AM (Exod. 3:14)—to Moses and calls Moses into the truth of who Moses is—the one sent to bring Israel out of Egypt.

If Moses was really *hearing* (*sh'ma*) what God had to say, the truth of who God is and who Moses was would have compelled him to appropriate action. But Moses, though grasping the words of God, was not *hearing* them in his heart.

We know this because he ultimately responds, "Please my Lord, send the message [of rescue to Israel] by [someone else]" (Exod. 4:13 AMP).

The God of Abraham, Isaac, and Jacob—the great I AM—announces to his friend Moses that his identity is "the one sent to draw Israel out of bondage," and Moses responds, "Send somebody else."

If we could pull Moses aside for a moment and ask, "What emotion is driving your decision-making process right now?" I'm guessing he would answer like most of us and say fear grounded in shame.

Moses might remind us of his last failed attempt at rescuing just one of his own Hebrew countrymen from an oppressive Egyptian and of his forty years in exile as a murderer. He went from a position of power and authority in the greatest kingdom of the day to being a sheep watcher at "the backside of the desert" (Exod. 3:1 KJV).

Now he's supposed to go deliver the entire nation? Get real!

Scripture tells us that when Moses heard and responded inappropriately to God's invitation, God's anger flared (see Exod. 4:14). God, in his great love for us, will never tolerate our believing the lies constantly being offered up to us by our own flesh, the world, and the Liar.

This wasn't about rule following. This was about Moses really hearing God—Moses allowing God's creative and infinitely powerful words to pierce his heart and show him the truth about who Moses was, about who God is. When truly hearing this truth, one cannot do anything but respond!

Unfortunately, we see with Moses that his false view of himself prevents him from really hearing and responding appropriately to the truth God is inviting him into; his false identity prevents him from living the life of thriving and purpose he was made to live.

That is because these lies prevent us from *hearing* (understanding and responding appropriately to) the truth about who we are and what we are here to do. If we allow them to, these lies can drown out what God is saying or suggest to us that the appropriate response to what God is telling us isn't necessary or what's best.

It is vital for our thriving that we lay down these lies about our identity, God, and the world and take up the truths that he is laying out for us. It is critical that—in big and small ways—we *hear* him and respond accordingly.

In what ways is your false view of yourself—however real the mistakes you've made in the past—diminishing your capacity to hear and respond appropriately to the God who calls you by name and whose Word is ready to slice through all the lies you've come to believe about yourself?

Attention

Slowly and intentionally read through the following passage three times. As you do, consider what words, phrases, or ideas God might be highlighting for you. Circle or underline what stands out to you, then answer the questions after the passage.

> "Therefore everyone who hears these words of mine and puts them into practice is like a wise man who built his house on the rock. The rain came down, the streams rose, and the winds blew and beat against that house; yet it did not fall, because it had its foundation on the rock. But everyone who hears these words of mine and does not put them into practice is like a foolish man who built his house on sand. The rain came down, the streams rose, and the winds blew and beat against that house, and it fell with a great crash."

> When Jesus had finished saying these things, the crowds were amazed at his teaching, because he taught as one who had authority, and not as their teachers of the law. (Matt. 7:24–29)

> After reading the passage above, what most stands out to you? What parts are confusing to you? What questions do you have?

In this, the final thought of the Sermon on the Mount, Jesus undoubtedly is hearkening back to the Hebrew understanding of *sh'ma*. Though using the Greek word *akouo*, Jesus makes known that it is not enough to simply listen to his words but that it is only the one who "puts them into practice" who avoids the devastation of the flood.

With the final thought of chapter 7, Matthew reminds his readers who Jesus is directly challenging through his teaching in the Sermon on the Mount: their teachers of the law. Throughout his sermon, Jesus throws down the gauntlet to those who are presenting the Jewish religious law—and life itself—as simply religious rule following.

Instead, Jesus presents a new way of approaching life—living with God in his kingdom in the fullness of who we are intended to be. This is contrasted with the life Jewish religious leaders were presenting—not a life of freedom but one of living under a strict religious code, trying to earn God's favor.

Jesus knew that this sort of rule following would only lead the people to ruin, as they would hear these commands but not allow them to truly bring about the obedient following of God that was intended. That is why Jesus called these teachers hypocrites, those who outwardly follow God but inwardly allow evil to rule in their hearts (see Matt. 23).

Life in the kingdom of God—the life of thriving we are intended for—involves an inward-to-outward transformation. We must truly *hear* the words of Jesus in our hearts if we are to respond appropriately, just as we know God hears and responds to us. As Jesus says in Matthew 7:7, "Ask and it will be given to you; seek and you will find; knock and the door will be opened to you."

We are being invited into a relationship of mutual listening and responding, one that is lived together in the power of God's foundational, transformational truth.

> Jesus, in light of or beyond the passage above, what is the most important thing you want to say to me right now?

> Jesus, why are you saying this to me? What do you want me to understand or see differently about myself, you, or the world?

Awareness

Prayerfully consider the last twenty-four hours—morning, afternoon, and evening—allowing yourself to become aware of Jesus's presence with you throughout the day. Chart out your day below.

	What situations, events, experiences, thoughts, and feelings is Jesus highlighting for me?	What does Jesus want to say to me about what he has highlighted?
MORNING		
AFTERNOON		
EVENING		

Considering what Jesus highlighted for you above, ask him how he was present with you throughout your day. How might he want you to notice him in similar situations in the future?

Annunciation

Ask Jesus the following questions, and write out the first thing he brings to your heart or mind.

Jesus, what aspect of my false identity am I holding on to that you want to highlight for me today?

> Jesus, how does that aspect of my false identity lead me to live from a place of fear? How does it awaken in me the desire to compete, compare, self-protect, and/or self-promote?

Pray the following prayer over yourself, lifting up and releasing to Jesus the aspect of your false self he has revealed to you.

Lord Jesus, as I give this aspect of my false identity to you, cleanse me of that lie and the fear it produces. I give it to you now, Christ Jesus. By the power of your life, death, and resurrection, I leave my burdens at the cross and take up your protection from and silencing of the enemy and all the false things in my life. As you bear this false identity in your own flesh, please exchange it within me for my true identity in you.

Next, ask Jesus the following questions about your true identity, again writing out the first thing he brings to your heart or mind.

> Jesus, in light of that false identity, would you speak back to me the name, or identity, that you call me? What do you want to reveal to me about my true identity today? What do you want to announce over me?

> Jesus, how would understanding this aspect of my true identity produce in me courage rather than fear? How would embracing this truth about who I am allow me to thrive in my life?

Pray the following prayer over yourself, holding in your heart and mind the aspect of your true self that Jesus has revealed to you.

Lord Jesus, when I give you my shame, you give me back honor. When I give you my guilt, you give me back innocence. When I give you my fear, you give me back power and authority. By the power of the cross, I claim the beautiful exchange of identity that you make possible for me. In your beautiful voice, Lord, I embrace the aspect of my true identity that you have made known to me today. Thank you for what you call me.

> Jesus, what one word or phrase do you want to leave me with today about my true identity?

Action

Use the following chart to prayerfully consider what Jesus might want to say to you (*"who hears these words of mine . . ."*) and how he wants you to respond to his words ("*. . . and puts them into practice*") over the next week. Consider sharing your planned responses with a trusted friend who can encourage you in following through. Also consider making this a regular practice to help you apply in your life what Jesus is revealing to you in prayer.

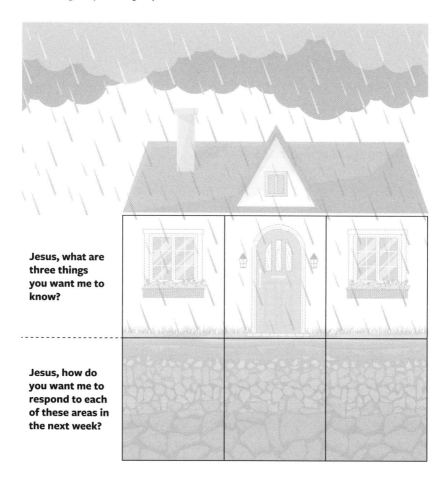

Note: This activity is about progress, not perfection. If you fail to put everything into practice over the next week, don't allow it to become a point of shame. (Shame will only serve to hold you back.) Simply talk about it with Jesus, asking him what prevented you from responding in the way you had planned. Next, ask him how you might follow through or if there are any adjustments that would be good for you to make to your response.

There are more of these "Hear and Put into Practice" pages in the back of this journal. Consider building this practice into a regular rhythm, using the pages until you have internalized the practice.

For Discussion or Further Reflection

What is significant to you about the Hebrew word for *hear*, *sh'ma*? How does this reframe your understanding of hearing God and obeying God?

When reading Matthew 7:24–29, what stands out to you about Jesus's illustration of the wise and foolish builders? How is the hearing that Jesus challenges us to different from what is commonly practiced both inside and outside the church?

When was a time that you were able to hear and put into practice something Jesus was teaching you? What was that experience like? How was it different from experiences in which you did not put Jesus's teaching into practice?

Where in your life do you feel that you have your "house built on the sand"? What might it look like to offer that area to Jesus, allowing your heart to truly hear his transformative words?

SESSION 10

STEPPING OUT IN FAITH

At one time, my family and I lived in Indonesia, where I was working as a peacemaker. While we were there the government collapsed. The military and the police simply disbanded, and angry mobs began looting and burning the city where we lived.

Unfortunately, or fortunately—however you look at it—we sensed from the Lord not to leave the country. Usually in these situations, foreign workers are the first ones out, which says something about our concern for the people of the country.

But the Lord said, "I want you to stay through this because I want your kids to see that I can protect them."

My wife, Donna, said, "Did he say we were included too, or just the kids?"

We stayed, and it was crazy. Thousands of people going up and down the streets, burning buildings and robbing people in all the big cities.

One time, we were driving down a quiet neighborhood street with our kids and some of their friends. We turned a corner and saw a mob of hundreds of people. They wore the headbands of an extremist political party. They were waving signs and sticks and broken bottles, screaming, chanting, and coming down the street, and there we were, a car full of foreigners.

And I couldn't back up!

Donna, suppressing the panic she felt, asked, "What should we do?"

Well, I didn't know. What *do* you do?

It didn't sound very spiritual, but I looked in the mirror and said to the kids, "Pray that we are invisible right now. Pray that God makes us invisible."

And my kids did just that. They became excited, raising their hands and repeating their prayer: "God, help us to be invisible, make us invisible."

As we prayed, I began to think that maybe this was a good idea after all. We didn't have sticks and broken glass, but we felt a surge of authority and power. Donna and I joined in, asking God to make us invisible to the mob.

The crowd came down the street to where we were, the only car in the middle of the road . . . and they went around us. They pushed against the car and shook it, but they didn't break any windows or beat the car or try to get in. The crowd flowed past, and we swayed like we were in a flood. This lasted for maybe five minutes because the crowd was so large.

We sat in the car, whispering, "Be invisible, be invisible," while the entire crowd went by. We were left unharmed and undamaged in the middle of the street.

I took a deep breath, sighed with relief, and had begun to drive when my oldest son yelled out, "Dad, don't drive yet. We're still invisible. God, make us visible again."

Can God still do stuff like that? Yes, he can.

But my family would not have believed in God's miraculous power to the same degree that we do now if we had never had that experience. We would not now trust in God's love and protection to the level that we do had we never followed him into that fearful situation in the first place.

That isn't to say that all of life will be as extreme as an angry mob enveloping your car, and my point definitely isn't to say that you should go out of your way to find such circumstances. (Remember, this was something God called us to do.)

Yet it is true that if we always try to avoid the difficult, uncomfortable, and scary stuff—the situations and people Jesus will often call us to—we will never truly experience the thriving life Jesus desires for us to have.

Sometimes as Christians it is easy to buy into the idea that the abundant life—the life Jesus has planned for each of us—consists of no struggle, challenge, or anxiety-inducing circumstances. When we experience these things, we are tempted to believe that we aren't doing Jesus-following the right way.

The truth is, however, that there is so much to be gained in such situations, so much Jesus can do in and through us when we step out in faith and follow him into something that is so far beyond anything we could overcome ourselves.

Sadly, fear often prevents most of us from ever experiencing such growth. It is not that we are able to avoid difficulties, risk, or fear—life drags us into these things regardless—but we cower in the face of it, not seeing how God desires to transform us in the midst of the struggle.

What would it look like instead to navigate the sometimes violent current of this life, allowing Jesus to guide and help us as we paddle and slice through these treacherous waters? We will find him to be not only an adequate guide but someone who is even able to command the river to bend to our ultimate good.

When we are willing to step out with God into unknown and uncomfortable territory, we really see how strong God is in the midst of our weakness. We start to see just how big our God really is. We also start to dream bigger, see far greater possibilities for our lives, and pursue our God-given purpose with courage, knowing that Jesus is by our side through it all.

That is where faith expands. That is where trust in God comes to full bloom within us. That is where thriving truly begins.

> When was a time that you stepped out into a difficult, uncomfortable, or scary situation and saw God show up in a powerful way? How was your faith in God strengthened through that experience?

Attention

Slowly and intentionally read through the following passage three times. As you do, consider what words, phrases, or ideas God might be highlighting for you. Circle or underline what stands out to you, then answer the questions after the passage.

> Therefore, since we are surrounded by so great a cloud of witnesses [who by faith have testified to the truth of God's absolute faithfulness], stripping off every unnecessary weight and the sin which so easily and cleverly entangles us, let us run with endurance and active persistence the race that is set before us, [looking away from all that will distract us and] focusing our eyes on Jesus, who is the Author and Perfecter of faith [the first incentive for our belief and the One who brings our faith to maturity], who for the joy [of accomplishing the goal] set before Him endured the cross, disregarding the shame, and sat down at the right hand of the throne of God [revealing His deity, His authority, and the completion of His work].
>
> Just consider and meditate on Him who endured from sinners such bitter hostility against Himself [consider it all in comparison with your trials], so that you will not grow weary and lose heart. (Heb. 12:1–3 AMP)

> After reading the passage above, what most stands out to you? What parts are confusing to you? What questions do you have?

Written originally for Jewish Christians, the book of Hebrews is a powerful exploration of how Jesus is the pinnacle of everything God has done and will ever do. Over and over again the author shows how all the stories of the Hebrew Scriptures (the Old Testament to us) pointed forward to Jesus as the ultimate revelation of God's love and life.

Coming into the final section of the letter, the author lays out in chapter 11 how all the luminaries of Israelite history stepped out *in faith*, following God into impossible and at times terrifying situations, trusting that in the end God would bring about the good he promised them.

Noah, Abraham, Sarah, Moses, Rahab, and more all took courageous steps of trust, believing that God would come through, even if the promise would not be fulfilled until after they had died. In this, they ultimately joined in on faith in God's plan of salvation, which would come through the future life, death, and resurrection of Jesus, God in the flesh. It is these luminaries that the author refers to in this passage as "so great a cloud of witnesses."

In light of all these faith-filled models, the readers are encouraged to "run with endurance and active persistence the race that is set before us." The image here presents the life God has planned for us as a race of a long distance. We are encouraged to endure and persist through difficulty, fear, and discomfort.

Another important point is that throughout the book of Hebrews, the author seems to suggest that these Jewish Christians are facing heavy persecution, causing some to walk away from faith in Jesus. The author implores them to keep their eyes on Jesus—like a runner keeps their eyes on the goal out in front of them—turning from distractions and shedding burdens and entangling sin.

In this, Jesus will not only author our faith (be the source of it) but also perfect it (or bring it to maturity). When we join Jesus, *considering and meditating* on him, trusting in him, and following him into the thriving life he has planned for us, we will discover the joy of running this race with endurance (see v. 2).

Like many athletes, we will find the fulfillment that comes from pushing past difficulty and struggle for the sake of an incredible goal. Except, where athletes push themselves to the brink of their own strength, we are to persevere in our trust in Jesus, stepping out in faith into impossible and at times terrifying situations, as he leads us into the incredible and purpose-filled thriving he has set before us.

> Jesus, in light of or beyond the passage above, what is the most important thing you want to say to me right now?

> Jesus, why are you saying this to me? What do you want me to understand or see differently about myself, you, or the world?

Awareness

Prayerfully consider the last twenty-four hours—morning, afternoon, and evening—allowing yourself to become aware of Jesus's presence with you throughout the day. Chart out your day below.

	What situations, events, experiences, thoughts, and feelings is Jesus highlighting for me?	What does Jesus want to say to me about what he has highlighted?
MORNING		
AFTERNOON		
EVENING		

Considering what Jesus highlighted for you above, ask him how he was present with you throughout your day. How might he want you to notice him in similar situations in the future?

Annunciation

Ask Jesus the following questions, and write out the first thing he brings to your heart or mind.

Jesus, what aspect of my false identity am I holding on to that you want to highlight for me today?

Jesus, how does that aspect of my false identity lead me to live from a place of fear? How does it awaken in me the desire to compete, compare, self-protect, and/or self-promote?

Pray the following prayer over yourself, lifting up and releasing to Jesus the aspect of your false self he has revealed to you.

Lord Jesus, as I give this aspect of my false identity to you, cleanse me of that lie and the fear it produces. I give it to you now, Christ Jesus. By the power of your life, death, and resurrection, I leave my burdens at the cross and take up your protection from and silencing of the enemy and all the false things in my life. As you bear this false identity in your own flesh, please exchange it within me for my true identity in you.

Next, ask Jesus the following questions about your true identity, again writing out the first thing he brings to your heart or mind.

> Jesus, in light of that false identity, would you speak back to me the name, or identity, that you call me? What do you want to reveal to me about my true identity today? What do you want to announce over me?

> Jesus, how would understanding this aspect of my true identity produce in me courage rather than fear? How would embracing this truth about who I am allow me to thrive in my life?

Pray the following prayer over yourself, holding in your heart and mind the aspect of your true self that Jesus has revealed to you.

Lord Jesus, when I give you my shame, you give me back honor. When I give you my guilt, you give me back innocence. When I give you my fear, you give me back power and authority. By the power of the cross, I claim the beautiful exchange of identity that you make possible for me. In your beautiful voice, Lord, I embrace the aspect of my true identity that you have made known to me today. Thank you for what you call me.

> Jesus, what one word or phrase do you want to leave me with today about my true identity?

Action

Go back and look through the "Annunciation" and "Action" sections in which God has revealed to you aspects of who he has made you to be. (In particular, look at the "Action" sections of sessions 1, 4, and 6.) Next, ask God the following, writing down what first comes to mind:

> Father, as I consider the journey you have been taking me on through this journal, what do you want me to notice about my identity?

Father, considering the true identity you created me to have and that you restored within me through Jesus, what do you want me to notice about the "race set before me" (i.e., my vocation[s], the things you have me here to do)?

Father, considering the vocation(s) you have planned for me—which flow from my true identity—where do you want me to step out in faith? What areas of fear, difficulty, or discomfort might you be calling me to follow you into?

Father, considering these places you desire for me to step into, how do you want to encourage me to persevere in this race? What do you want to tell me in regard to the fear, difficulty, or discomfort I will face? How do you want to transform these experiences into something else inside of me?

Father, as I move forward with you, help me to endure as I keep my eyes on Jesus, the Beginner and Finisher of this race of faith I am running. Thank you for the identity and purpose you have given me. Transform my fear into courage as I follow you into places that are scary, uncomfortable, and at times involve great difficulty. Guide me as I run in step with Jesus's Spirit. Amen.

For Discussion or Further Reflection

How have you seen endurance in faith play a role in your own life or the life of someone you know? What did you notice about your/their connection to Jesus during that time?

When reading Hebrews 12:1–3, what areas do you think are important to address if one is to endure? What do you think it means to keep our eyes focused on Jesus?

What does it look like, practically, to consider and meditate on Jesus and his own endurance? How might this serve you in building endurance to do what Jesus is calling you to do (the race set out before you), even in the midst of difficulty?

What is one area where you feel like you are struggling to endure in your faith in Jesus? How might you introduce a practice of prayerfully considering and meditating on Jesus?

SESSION 11

WHEN WE NEED WISDOM

Once, after a particularly devastating setback in a Middle Eastern country, which resulted in our arrest and expulsion from that country, a friend called to check on our well-being and offer encouragement.

After listening to me recount the circumstances surrounding the event—the betrayal, the failure, and the resulting sense of fear, guilt, and shame—his advice was simple: "Well, God still speaks and his word still cuts, so let's ask God what he wants you to know and what he wants you to do."

How often do we forget this astounding truth, that we worship the God who speaks? He still speaks and his word still cuts—two often-neglected facts that help protect us from bad decisions, wrong conclusions, and just overall faulty thinking.

Remembering this is vital if we are to persevere in the thriving life Jesus has for each of us.

At that seemingly inescapable low point in my walk with the Lord—being arrested and expelled from a country—I remembered the words of James, the brother of Jesus, in his letter to the Jews who were dispersed throughout the non-Jewish world: "If any of you is deficient in wisdom, let him ask of the giving God [Who gives] to everyone liberally and ungrudgingly, without reproaching or faultfinding, and it will be given him" (James 1:5 AMPC).

Deficient in wisdom? I feel as if I'm regularly lacking in wisdom. What's the solution? Ask.

And please note that the one you are asking is no distant, petulant, capricious god of our own invention, who cannot help and leads us astray. Instead, we are calling on the One who spoke creation—that includes us—into existence and calls us by name. This is the God of Abraham, Isaac, and Jacob, the God and Father of our Lord Jesus Christ, who gives wisdom (Greek *sophia*—"broad and full of intelligence; used of the knowledge of very diverse matters"[1]) liberally without reproach or faultfinding.

God is ready and willing to lavish his wisdom all over us if we will only ask. In addition to his willingness to pour out this wisdom, God's wisdom covers every discipline of human endeavor. We need only to inquire of him.

Even Jesus, being fully human, grew in wisdom (see Luke 2:52) and trusted in the Father to guide everything he said and did (see John 5:30). Jesus modeled for us human thriving and the highest level of knowing—asking wisdom from the God who speaks!

Think of it from this perspective: Jesus isn't so much teaching people what to do in a given situation as he is teaching them *how to know what to do in every situation*—ask and keep on asking, seek and keep on seeking, knock and keep on knocking (see Matt. 7:7–11 AMP).

This is a vital area of our thriving, that in the midst of what feels like failure, we recognize that, even there, God is speaking to us. That who we

---

1. Bible Study Tools, s.v. "sophia (n.)," New Testament Greek Lexicon, accessed June 14, 2024, https://www.biblestudytools.com/lexicons/greek/nas/sophia.html.

are and what we are here to do cannot be separated from the voice of our heavenly Father guiding, encouraging, and correcting each of our steps.

There will be moments as you pursue your vocation when things do not work out the way you had imagined or hoped. In these moments it is tempting to despair and question if you were really following God in the first place. It is easy to want to quit or take on an easier (albeit less fulfilling) life.

In these times it is vital to come back to Father God with the essential questions of the thriver: God, what do you want me to know/feel/do in this situation? What wisdom do you want to impart to me? What do you have for me in this challenging situation? What lies do you want me to put down? What truths shall I take up?

Jesus, what are you up to now?

> Describe a difficult time—when you were confused as to what God was doing and what you were to do—when God gave you wisdom to make it through. What made that time so difficult? How did that wisdom help?

Attention

Slowly and intentionally read through the following passage three times. As you do, consider what words, phrases, or ideas God might be highlighting for you. Circle or underline what stands out to you, then answer the questions after the passage.

Dear brothers and sisters, when troubles of any kind come your way, consider it an opportunity for great joy. For you know that when your faith is tested, your endurance has a chance to grow. So let it grow, for when your endurance is fully developed, you will be perfect and complete, needing nothing.

If you need wisdom, ask our generous God, and he will give it to you. He will not rebuke you for asking. But when you ask him, be sure that your faith is in God alone. Do not waver, for a person with divided loyalty is as unsettled as a wave of the sea that is blown and tossed by the wind. Such people should not expect to receive anything from the Lord. Their loyalty is divided between God and the world, and they are unstable in everything they do. (James 1:2–8 NLT)

> After reading the passage above, what most stands out to you? What parts are confusing to you? What questions do you have?

Again, we are looking at the theme of endurance in our faith in Jesus (a regular drumbeat of the New Testament writers). But this time we're approaching endurance from a slightly different angle—wisdom.

The book of James was written by an early leader in the first church in Jerusalem who was actually the half brother of Jesus. This book was written shortly before James was martyred, and it contains a ton of wisdom about what it means to follow Jesus wholeheartedly.

This passage is part of James's introduction to this wisdom teaching and lays the groundwork for everything he is about to say. He starts in an interesting place, encouraging his readers to reframe "troubles of any kind" as "an opportunity for great joy."

It's interesting that a book of wisdom should start this way. James seems to suggest that this understanding of life and its difficulties is where wisdom begins to grow and how Jesus ultimately makes us *perfect and complete*. The word translated "perfect" here is the Greek word *teleios*, and it carries with it the idea that we are whole and undivided—that we are consistent between who we are (our true identity in Christ) and what we do (our vocation flowing from that identity).

Throughout this work, it is this consistency of self that James presents as vital to the life of true thriving, pointing out how "faith by itself, if it is not accompanied by action, is dead" (2:17). James makes clear that the obvious conclusion of someone truly and wholeheartedly trusting in Jesus will always be the action-based love of God and neighbor.

It is in this context that we are encouraged to ask for wisdom about our specific situations, allowing that wisdom to steer us back to faith in Jesus no matter our circumstances, from which love will inevitably bloom.

Hearkening back to the *teleios* Jesus is bringing about in us, we are challenged not to be "a person with divided loyalty," fractured between our trust in God and the things of this world that claim to steady us. There is no true joy to be found in these worldly things, only instability. James uses the image of being unanchored in a wild and unruly sea, this life and its troubles easily tossing us this way and that.

Instead, we are encouraged to ask God for his wisdom as a way of anchoring us to him and the growth that he brings about in this life. Then, in our faith, joy, and love, we can endure and thrive in the life he has planned for us.

Jesus, in light of or beyond the passage above, what is the most important thing you want to say to me right now?

Jesus, why are you saying this to me? What do you want me to understand or see differently about myself, you, or the world?

Awareness

Prayerfully consider the last twenty-four hours—morning, afternoon, and evening—allowing yourself to become aware of Jesus's presence with you throughout the day. Chart out your day below.

	What situations, events, experiences, thoughts, and feelings is Jesus highlighting for me?	What does Jesus want to say to me about what he has highlighted?
MORNING		
AFTERNOON		
EVENING		

Considering what Jesus highlighted for you above, ask him how he was present with you throughout your day. How might he want you to notice him in similar situations in the future?

Annunciation

Ask Jesus the following questions, and write out the first thing he brings to your heart or mind.

Jesus, what aspect of my false identity am I holding on to that you want to highlight for me today?

Jesus, how does that aspect of my false identity lead me to live from a place of fear? How does it awaken in me the desire to compete, compare, self-protect, and/or self-promote?

Pray the following prayer over yourself, lifting up and releasing to Jesus the aspect of your false self he has revealed to you.

Lord Jesus, as I give this aspect of my false identity to you, cleanse me of that lie and the fear it produces. I give it to you now, Christ Jesus. By the power of your life, death, and resurrection, I leave my burdens at the cross and take up your protection from and silencing of the enemy and all the false things in my life. As you bear this false identity in your own flesh, please exchange it within me for my true identity in you.

Next, ask Jesus the following questions about your true identity, again writing out the first thing he brings to your heart or mind.

> Jesus, in light of that false identity, would you speak back to me the name, or identity, that you call me? What do you want to reveal to me about my true identity today? What do you want to announce over me?

> Jesus, how would understanding this aspect of my true identity produce in me courage rather than fear? How would embracing this truth about who I am allow me to thrive in my life?

Pray the following prayer over yourself, holding in your heart and mind the aspect of your true self that Jesus has revealed to you.

Lord Jesus, when I give you my shame, you give me back honor. When I give you my guilt, you give me back innocence. When I give you my fear, you give me back power and authority. By the power of the cross, I claim the beautiful exchange of identity that you make possible for me. In your beautiful voice, Lord, I embrace the aspect of my true identity that you have made known to me today. Thank you for what you call me.

> Jesus, what one word or phrase do you want to leave me with today about my true identity?

Action

Let's do a visual exercise. For this activity you will need **five cups or glasses**, a **pitcher or large container**, some **sticky notes**, and a bag of **dry beans** (or a good number of any small objects, like M&Ms, popcorn kernels, marbles, or even paper clips).

1. Start by sticking to each of the five cups or glasses a sticky note that identifies each cup as one of the five areas in which you most need wisdom in your life right now. It could be something to do with work, a specific relationship, a difficult decision you have to make, how to handle a particular area of struggle or sin, etc. There is no need to overthink it. Just prayerfully

consider which five areas of life you most need God's wisdom in. Also put a sticky note that reads "God" on the pitcher or large container.

2. Next, divide the beans (or other small objects) between the five cups. Prayerfully consider each area in which you need wisdom, giving more beans to the areas that weigh on you most and fewer beans to the areas that are weighing on you least. Do this until you have distributed the whole bag of beans across the five cups.

3. Once finished, take each cup in your hand and ask, *Father, where am I putting my trust other than in you when it comes to this area of my life?* For each cup, write down what you hear in the space provided below.

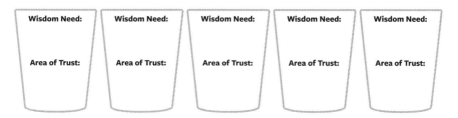

4. Finally, after putting the pitcher, or container representing God, at the center of the five cups, take one bean at a time (starting with the cup with the fewest beans) and begin to drop them into the pitcher in the center. As you do, ask God for wisdom in that specific area, declaring your trust in him. Once you have finished transferring all the beans out of one cup and into the pitcher, pause a moment and write in the space below what you heard God say in regard to that area of your life. Then move on to the next cup and the next until all the beans have been moved to the pitcher representing God. The goal is to slow down and

really listen for God in each of these areas, so take your time, focusing your attention on what God wants to say to you.

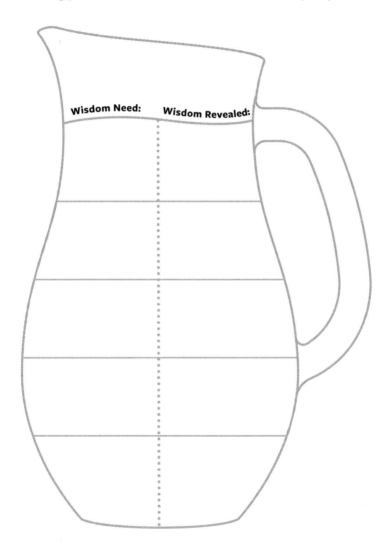

Wisdom Need: **Wisdom Revealed:**

5. Afterward, spend some time asking God how you might apply each area of wisdom in your life.

For Discussion or Further Reflection

What are the hallmarks of a person with divided loyalty? In contrast, how would you describe someone who is whole, unfractured, and fully integrated in their loyalty?

Considering James 1:2–8, how can asking for God's wisdom steady us in the midst of trouble? How can having your faith divided among many areas (not in God alone) cause you to experience unsteadiness in the face of troubles?

Where in your life do you feel divided in your faith? What areas do you look to other than God to steady you in times of trouble?

How might God be calling you to shift your trust in these areas back to him? How might asking for wisdom in these areas help you to that end?

SESSION 12

DISCOVERING YOUR MISSION

Some time ago, I met a man named Jerry. He was a massive, athletic forty-five-year-old man who had just come to Christ.

As a new believer, Jerry still struggled with anger and violence. Life experiences had made him quite hostile. I started meeting with Jerry and walking with him through his challenges in his new relationship with Jesus.

I asked him his story and he told me that when he was young, he was physically bigger than other kids. His dad and his neighbor said, "You ought to play rugby." The problem was, he didn't want to play rugby because he wasn't mean; he was actually quite tenderhearted. Rugby, however, was important to his dad, so his dad kept making him play rugby junior league and then on into secondary school.

Every time he played, the coaches would say, "You gotta get mad. You're too nice out there. You gotta get mad." Consequently, he started taking on this identity of being angry on the field because he didn't want to play in the first place. But when he got mad, he succeeded, and he received a lot of accolades.

He went through high school and he was really good, and he got really big and he became really mean. Therefore, he was awarded a university scholarship to play rugby, but he hated playing the game. He accepted the scholarship in order to attend university, and his identity became the big, mean, angry rugby guy.

In his second year, he was severely injured. As a result, he couldn't play and lost his scholarship. But his scholarship status had made passing grades automatic, so he'd never had to study. Therefore, he also considered himself stupid.

Now he saw himself as big and mean and not smart. He was no longer a rugby star. What was he? Big, mean, angry, and unsure what to do. So he fought people. He fought and he got arrested often and he got a girl pregnant. His life turned into a protracted, violent disaster.

Then he met Jesus and began to live in the kingdom of God. But the anger didn't just go away like magic, so he asked me, "What do I do with this intense anger?"

I said, "I don't know, but I know how to know." We began meeting and praying together.

During the prayer process, I asked the Lord to reveal to Jerry the first time he felt this level of anger in his life and what the source of this anger was.

Jerry remembered his first feeling of anger as being on the rugby field as a youth. He didn't like playing rugby, but his dad kept telling him he was weak and a coward if he didn't want to play sports. The whole scenario made Jerry feel like a disappointment to his dad. It gave him an identity of unworthiness.

In this identity, Jerry's anger rose up to protect him and help him succeed in the false self. This was the source of his pain and where the Lord wanted to meet him—on the day Jerry began to believe that lie. The Lord was with Jerry on that day.

Jerry recalled a particularly humiliating incident with his father. As we prayed through the memory, Jerry sensed the Lord saying, "I made you to be a counselor to people."

When Jerry heard this, he began to cry. This big, angry man started to cry and said, "I think God says I'm his counselor."

"What kind of counselor?" I asked.

"A family counselor."

Really? Wow. What a history for that. It makes sense. But what did the enemy want Jerry to fear and avoid? His true identity. When the Lord says, "You're my family counselor," the enemy will immediately challenge with, "Really, you? Impossible."

This is why it is so beneficial to be in a community of trusted believers when you are hearing from the Lord.

When our small group found out that God called Jerry a family counselor, we all encouraged him and held him accountable to becoming a family counselor. This is the definition of true accountability—affirming and nudging people forward in their true identity and destiny.

With the support of his community, Jerry realized that pursuing this vocation would be the most redemptive thing he could ever do or imagine.

That is what Jesus does.

Who understands family tragedy more than Jerry? Who understands anger in a family more than Jerry? Jesus was bringing about redemption in the midst of his story, showing him that with God none of these experiences would be wasted.

To encourage him on his journey, our community rallied around him and stood by him through two years of college, where he finished with honors. With continued support from his community, Jerry then completed his counseling degree while volunteering at his local church in the counseling program. During these years, Jerry also reconciled with his wife and children.

Although Jerry had wandered for forty-five years, lost in a false identity, these opportune moments in his life didn't pass him by; they never moved. As Jerry moved forward in his true identity, these moments came into view and he walked right into them.

He found God's mission for his life had always been within reach. He only needed the eyes to see it right in front of him.

As we wrap up our time walking together through this journal, I want you to know that your destiny and purpose are right there if you are willing to walk each day in the right direction in your true identity.

By fostering a life of abiding in Jesus as a loved child of God—through attention, awareness, annunciation, and action—we can find the life that we were always intended for, a life of joy, hope, love, and purpose. A life of understanding who we are (our identity) and what we are here to do (our vocation).

In this, we thrive.

> As you consider your walk through this journal, what destiny or mission might God be making you aware of? How does that destiny or mission flow from your God-given identity?

Attention

Slowly and intentionally read through the following passage three times. As you do, consider what words, phrases, or ideas God might be highlighting for you. Circle or underline what stands out to you, then answer the questions after the passage.

> It was in the year King Uzziah died that I saw the Lord. He was sitting on a lofty throne, and the train of his robe filled the Temple. Attending him were mighty seraphim, each having six wings. With two wings they covered their faces, with two they covered their feet, and with two they flew. They were calling out to each other,
>
>> "Holy, holy, holy is the LORD of Heaven's Armies!
>> The whole earth is filled with his glory!"
>
> Their voices shook the Temple to its foundations, and the entire building was filled with smoke.
> Then I said, "It's all over! I am doomed, for I am a sinful man. I have filthy lips, and I live among a people with filthy lips. Yet I have seen the King, the LORD of Heaven's Armies."
> Then one of the seraphim flew to me with a burning coal he had taken from the altar with a pair of tongs. He touched my lips with it and said, "See, this coal has touched your lips. Now your guilt is removed, and your sins are forgiven."
> Then I heard the Lord asking, "Whom should I send as a messenger to this people? Who will go for us?"
> I said, "Here I am. Send me." (Isa. 6:1–8 NLT)

After reading the passage above, what most stands out to you? What parts are confusing to you? What questions do you have?

This passage recounts an incredible vision of God that a man named Isaiah had. This is the moment that Isaiah is sent into his vocation, his life's mission, to speak as a prophet (a person commissioned to speak to the people on God's behalf).

In this vision, Isaiah is brought before God and faced with God's incredible holiness (the quality of being set apart and above everything else) and glory (the quality of rich and indescribable splendor and honor). In the face of such a God, Isaiah is instantly made aware of how incredibly short he and all of Israel fall of who they are intended to be—how short they fall of their intended identity to be a people set apart as a blessing to the rest of the world.

Then something pretty interesting happens: a seraphim—a type of angel—brings a hot coal to Isaiah's lips. Instead of burning Isaiah, it acts as a purifying fire, helping Isaiah—a man of "filthy lips"—become the mouthpiece of God he was always intended to be.

This theme of refining fire is visited time and time again throughout the book of Isaiah as he warns Israel of how their idolatry and injustice will lead to their ultimate downfall. But like the burning coal on Isaiah's lips, the fire that will light Israel ablaze (in the form of being conquered and exiled by a foreign army) will not end in consumption but will serve as Israel's eventual refinement. It will guide them back toward taking up their true God-given identity.

God speaks of Israel as a stump that has been chopped down and burned but also declares that that charred stump will ultimately serve as a "holy seed" (see 6:13), and a new branch will sprout from "the stump of the line of Jesse" (see 11:1), King David's father. This new shoot represents Jesus, the future Messiah-King, through whom Israel will again take up their true identity as a blessing to the world.

Isaiah, being restored to his God-given identity, cannot help but respond to God's call by crying out, "Here I am. Send me." This is because in our restored identity we are compelled to live worship-filled lives of thriving, responding to God's holiness and glory with all that we have and are.

In this, we find our truest vocation, our life's mission, the outpouring of our God-given identity that cannot be contained.

In the face of God's glory and in our restored identity, we too cannot help but respond, *Here I am. Send me.*

> Jesus, in light of or beyond the passage above, what is the most important thing you want to say to me right now?

> Jesus, why are you saying this to me? What do you want me to understand or see differently about myself, you, or the world?

Awareness

Prayerfully consider the last twenty-four hours—morning, afternoon, and evening—allowing yourself to become aware of Jesus's presence with you throughout the day. Chart out your day below.

	What situations, events, experiences, thoughts, and feelings is Jesus highlighting for me?	*What does Jesus want to say to me about what he has highlighted?*
MORNING		
AFTERNOON		
EVENING		

Considering what Jesus highlighted for you above, ask him how he was present with you throughout your day. How might he want you to notice him in similar situations in the future?

Annunciation

Ask Jesus the following questions, and write out the first thing he brings to your heart or mind.

Jesus, what aspect of my false identity am I holding on to that you want to highlight for me today?

Jesus, how does that aspect of my false identity lead me to live from a place of fear? How does it awaken in me the desire to compete, compare, self-protect, and/or self-promote?

Pray the following prayer over yourself, lifting up and releasing to Jesus the aspect of your false self he has revealed to you.

> *Lord Jesus, as I give this aspect of my false identity to you, cleanse me of that lie and the fear it produces. I give it to you now, Christ Jesus. By the power of your life, death, and resurrection, I leave my burdens at the cross and take up your protection from and silencing of the enemy and all the false things in my life. As you bear this false identity in your own flesh, please exchange it within me for my true identity in you.*

Next, ask Jesus the following questions about your true identity, again writing out the first thing he brings to your heart or mind.

> Jesus, in light of that false identity, would you speak back to me the name, or identity, that you call me? What do you want to reveal to me about my true identity today? What do you want to announce over me?

> Jesus, how would understanding this aspect of my true identity produce in me courage rather than fear? How would embracing this truth about who I am allow me to thrive in my life?

Pray the following prayer over yourself, holding in your heart and mind the aspect of your true self that Jesus has revealed to you.

Lord Jesus, when I give you my shame, you give me back honor. When I give you my guilt, you give me back innocence. When I give you my fear, you give me back power and authority. By the power of the cross, I claim the beautiful exchange of identity that you make possible for me. In your beautiful voice, Lord, I embrace the aspect of my true identity that you have made known to me today. Thank you for what you call me.

> Jesus, what one word or phrase do you want to leave me with today about my true identity?

Action

Take some time to prayerfully consider all that God has revealed to you across the sessions of this journal, asking:

> Jesus, what do you want me to hold on to most about the journey you have taken me on over the course of this journal?

Next, prayerfully consider how you would finish the following two sentences given all God has revealed to you during this journey. Feel free to use a word, phrase, or several words to describe the true identity and vocation revealed to you by God throughout this process.

My God-given <u>identity</u> is . . .

My identity-fueled <u>vocation</u> is . . .

Finally, take some time to brainstorm with God as to what your life's mission statement might be. Make it one memorable sentence that is reflective of both your identity and vocation but sends you out into the life of thriving you were intended for.

Imagine yourself responding to this mission with the words, **Here I am. Send me!**

My life's God-given <u>mission</u> is to . . .

Note: This mission statement is a starting place. God will likely shape and refine it further over the course of the years as you grow more and more into your identity and vocation. Take it seriously, but also leave room for it to develop as you develop.

For Discussion or Further Reflection

Who is someone you have known or know of who lives life with a God-given mission? What about their life is distinct and noteworthy?

When reading about Isaiah's vision, what in particular stands out to you? What do you think changed in Isaiah, causing his response to God to shift from the beginning of the vision to the end?

Where might God want to redeem your story for the sake of the mission he has for your life? How would you be forced to fully rely on God in this area?

Considering the mission God helped you develop in the "Action" section of this session, what action steps might you take over the coming weeks to continue pursuing this calling? Over the coming months? Over the coming years?

Final Note

As I said at the beginning of our time together, this journal is merely a tool through which you might engage the living Spirit of Jesus, who is dwelling inside you and through whom your identity is created and restored and your vocation is realized. Without Jesus, these pages are a cold piece of wire, unable to conduct any power on their own.

That said, I pray that the space between these two covers continues to be a meeting place for you and your Lord. Many of the practices, prayers, and teachings found here take time to fully root themselves in our hearts, lives, and rhythms. Come back often to reengage with Jesus and the work he started in you here. Let this be a trellis on which you grow and learn to abide in the One who will lead you toward the life of thriving you were always intended for.

This might mean going through this material twice, three times, or ten times, but I trust that as you grow in strength, you will look around and realize this journal is no longer necessary, that the principles and practices of this journey with Jesus are ingrained within you—that abiding in him is second nature.

This, of course, will not mean that you have "arrived." None of us will be our fullest selves this side of Jesus's return. But we can be "certain that God, who began the good work within you, will continue his work until it is finally finished on the day when Christ Jesus returns" (Phil. 1:6 NLT). Until then, let us take up the abundant life Jesus offers us in the here and now.

Until then, let us live as those who thrive.

Confession Pages

In the space provided, spend some time going through a practice of confession with God, centering yourself on the following passage:

> If we confess our sins, he is faithful and just and will forgive us our sins and purify us from all unrighteousness. (1 John 1:9)

> *Father God, thank you for loving and forgiving me by the power of your Son, Jesus Christ. Thank you for purifying me from my unrighteous acts, words, thoughts, and beliefs. I confess that I have been sinful—that I have missed the mark of who you have made me to be and what you have for me to do here on earth.*
>
> *Father God, bring to mind anything and everything that would be good for me to confess—whether I've recognized it as sin or not—all the while reminding me that my shame has been put to death with Jesus on the cross.*

~ ~ ~

*Father, what **actions** do I need to tell you the truth about today?*

Thank you for your forgiveness, Father.

*Father, what **thoughts** do I need to tell you the truth about today?*

Thank you for your forgiveness, Father.

*Father, what **words** do I need to tell you the truth about today?*

Thank you for your forgiveness, Father.

*Father, what **beliefs**—about you, myself, or others—do I need to tell you the truth about today?*

Thank you for your forgiveness, Father.

*Father, what does **repentance** look like today? (What is one way I can turn from my false identity and live from my true self today?)*

Father, thank you for purifying me in the name of your Son, Jesus Christ, and by the power of his life, death, and resurrection. Amen.

Confession Pages

*Father, what **actions** do I need to tell you the truth about today?*

Thank you for your forgiveness, Father.

*Father, what **thoughts** do I need to tell you the truth about today?*

Thank you for your forgiveness, Father.

*Father, what **words** do I need to tell you the truth about today?*

Thank you for your forgiveness, Father.

*Father, what **beliefs**—about you, myself, or others—do I need to tell you the truth about today?*

Thank you for your forgiveness, Father.

*Father, what does **repentance** look like today? (What is one way I can turn from my false identity and live from my true self today?)*

Father, thank you for purifying me in the name of your Son, Jesus Christ, and by the power of his life, death, and resurrection. Amen.

*Father, what **actions** do I need to tell you the truth about today?*

Thank you for your forgiveness, Father.

*Father, what **thoughts** do I need to tell you the truth about today?*

Thank you for your forgiveness, Father.

*Father, what **words** do I need to tell you the truth about today?*

Thank you for your forgiveness, Father.

*Father, what **beliefs**—about you, myself, or others—do I need to tell you the truth about today?*

Thank you for your forgiveness, Father.

*Father, what does **repentance** look like today? (What is one way I can turn from my false identity and live from my true self today?)*

Father, thank you for purifying me in the name of your Son, Jesus Christ, and by the power of his life, death, and resurrection. Amen.

Hear and Put into Practice

Use the following chart to prayerfully consider what Jesus might want to say to you (*"hears these words of mine . . ."*) and how he wants you to respond to his words (*". . . and puts them into practice"*) over the next week. Consider sharing your planned responses with a trusted friend who can encourage you in following through. Also consider making this a regular practice to help you to apply in your life what Jesus is revealing to you in prayer.

Remember: This activity is about progress, not perfection. If you fail to put everything into practice over the next week, simply talk about it with Jesus, asking him what prevented you from responding the way you had planned. Next, ask him how you might follow through or if there are any adjustments to your response that would be good for you to make.

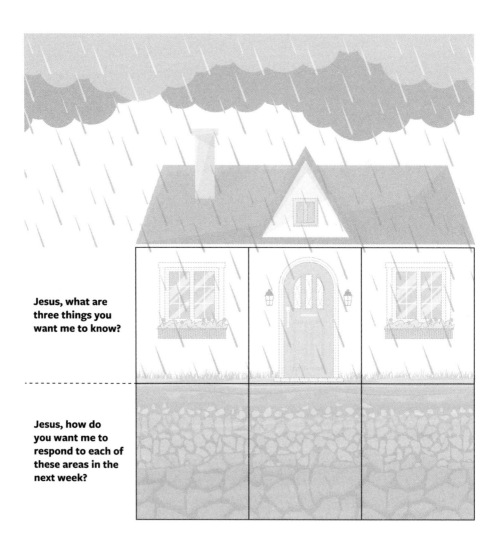

Jesus, what are three things you want me to know?

Jesus, how do you want me to respond to each of these areas in the next week?

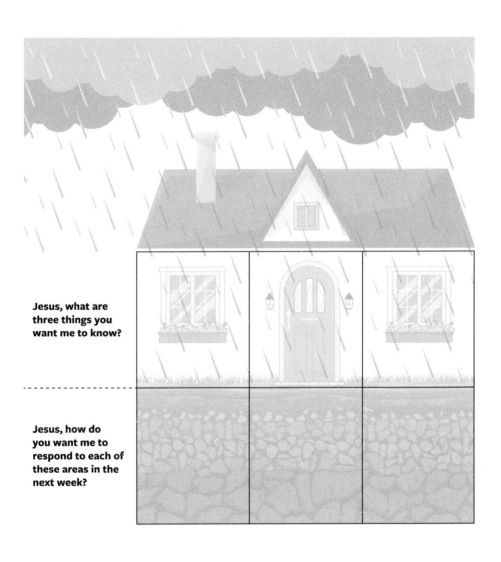

Jesus, what are three things you want me to know?

Jesus, how do you want me to respond to each of these areas in the next week?

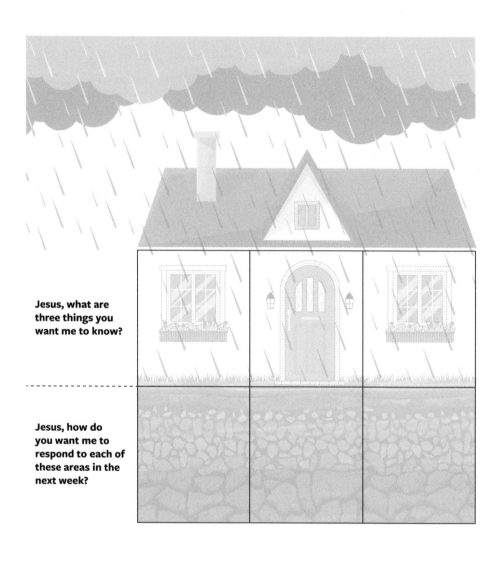

Jesus, what are three things you want me to know?

Jesus, how do you want me to respond to each of these areas in the next week?

Jamie Winship is a former Metro DC area police officer who spent nearly thirty years living and working in the Muslim world, teaching people how to hear from God and live in his kingdom. Jamie and his wife, Donna, speak around the US and across the globe to help people find their God-given identity and experience a life of freedom. Jamie and Donna live in East Tennessee.

Connect with Jamie:

IdentityExchange.com

@IdentityExchange

A Note from the Publisher

Dear Reader,

Thank you for selecting a Revell book! We're so happy to be part of your life through this work.

Revell's mission is to publish books that offer hope and help for meeting life's challenges, and that that bring comfort and inspiration. We know that the right words at the right time can make all the difference; it is our goal with every title to provide just the words you need.

We believe in building lasting relationships with readers, and we'd love to get to know you better. If you have any feedback, questions, or just want to chat about your experience reading this book, please email us directly at publisher@revellbooks.com. Your insights are incredibly important to us, and it would be our pleasure to hear how we can better serve you.

We look forward to hearing from you and having the chance to enhance your experience with Revell Books.

The Publishing Team at Revell Books
A Division of Baker Publishing Group
publisher@revellbooks.com